To

. . . .

From

. . . .

A Woman's Heart: Devotions for Women by Women
Copyright © 2018 by Worthy Inspired

ISBN: 9781683972440

Published by Worthy Inspired, an imprint of Worthy Publishing Group,
a division of Worthy Media, Inc., One Franklin Park, 6100 Tower Circle,
Suite 210, Franklin, TN 37067.

WORTHY is a registered trademark of Worthy Media, Inc.

HELPING PEOPLE EXPERIENCE THE HEART OF GOD.

Library of Congress Control Number: 2017960760

All Scripture quotations, unless otherwise indicated, are taken from the
Holy Bible, *New International Version®, NIV®*. Copyright © 1973, 1978,
1984 by Biblica, Inc.™ Used by permission of Zondervan. All rights
reserved worldwide.

Packaged by Worthy Media. For subsidiary and foreign language rights
contact info@worthymedia.com

Produced with the assistance of The Livingstone Corporation
(www.LivingstoneCorp.com).

Cover design: Melissa Reagan
Art: iStockPhoto.com
Interior Design and Typesetting: Bart Dawson

Printed in China

18 19 20 21 22 23 RRD 11 10 9 8 7 6 5 4 3 2

A
Woman's
Heart

Devotions for Women
by Women

WORTHY®
Inspired

Welcome

*A*cross the centuries and around the world, remarkable Christian women have been writing. Whether by candlelight with a quill pen or on the latest laptop computer, women have shared comfort, inspiration, admonition, and biblical insight. Writing from their personal experiences and lessons learned from in-depth study, they offer their hearts to us, with enormous riches to share.

A Woman's Heart is a collection of devotions inspired by little nuggets of wisdom gleaned from Christian women writers across the centuries. From these writings, we've chosen powerful, one- or two-sentence quotations that will provide a spark in your personal walk with God. Each seed quotation is followed by a longer devotion, a suggested Scripture reading, and a short prayer starter.

As you take a few minutes from your busy day to enjoy God's presence, may you be drawn closer to Him and be able to say in humble submission, "Take my heart, O God."

The Editors

Contributors

Cheryl Dunlop

Heather Pleier

Carol Fielding

Kathy Hardee

Peggy Billiard

Sue Rosenfeld

Judith Costello

Diane Markins

Michelle Van Loon

Brenda Nixon

Kathy Lay

Drenda Thomas Richards

Linda McGee

Pat Stockett Johnston

Mary Grace Birkhead

Sandra Stein

Gail Krahenbuhl

Debbie Simler-Goff

Linda Washington

Betsy Schmitt

Linda Taylor

God of All Comfort

*Among all the names that reveal God, this,
the "God of all comfort," seems to me one of the loveliest
and the most absolutely comforting. The words all comfort
admit of no limitations and no deductions.*

Hannah Whitall Smith

We love seeing the word *all* if it points to something favorable for us. We love when all the shoes at our favorite store are on sale, or all the candies in the bowl are dark chocolate, or all the bills are paid in full. However, when all aspects of life seem to crash down around us, that's a different matter. We find ourselves in desperate need of the "God of *all* comfort."

Consider the ramifications of that name. No problem or heartache is outside of God's range of comfort. He has unlimited resources—a vast wellspring—at His disposal. When we're hurting, truly the loveliest name of all describes God bringing us, not *some* comfort, not comfort for *some* things, but *all* the comfort we need.

The God of all comfort waits today to comfort you. No limitations. No deductions.

Read 2 Corinthians 1:3–5.

God of all comfort, I need Your comfort right now.

More Like Jesus

God has chosen you and me for the purpose
of bearing much eternal fruit . . . fruit that is simply
the character of God's Son coming out in us.
Anne Graham Lotz

*H*ow often do you find yourself feeling melancholy, looking back with some regret or ahead with fearful questions? Issues and anxiety don't leave much room for hope. Certainly, you *want* to feel optimistic, even joyful, but how?

The answer comes not in trying, but knowing; not in doing, but in resting. In Galatians 5, God promises joy as a fruit of His work in us. So instead of trying to manufacture a feeling of joy, look to your Father in heaven and remember His promise. He has already planted joy in your heart by His Spirit. So *feeling* joyful is not the issue. Instead, sit quietly before God and express to Him your deepest hurts and concerns; ask Him to grow in you His fruit of joy. Then, as Anne says, you will continue to bear fruit—eternal fruit—for Him, daily becoming more like His Son.

Read Galatians 5:22–23.

Lord, help my life show the fruit of the Spirit
in everything I do today.

Hungry Soul

*O faithful soul! The repose enjoyed in thyself is
but a shadow of that which thou wilt find in God!*

Madame Guyon

Rest. Repose. Times of quiet when we can think—about God, about life, about what we are called to do. Such times grant us refreshment, a needed break, a time to refocus.

And yet, Madame Guyon would have us realize that those precious times are mere shadows of the rest that our souls can find in God.

Our souls thirst; He alone can satisfy. We hunger to know the depths of God's love; He fills us to overflowing with nourishment from His Word. We face difficult times; He gives us the refreshment that keeps us moving forward. We struggle with guilt over sins we have committed; He alone grants us forgiveness that brings true peace and repose. We need rest from the storm; He invites us into His refuge and wraps His arms of protection around us.

Today, let your soul find its best rest in Him.

Read Psalm 62:5–8.

Lord Jesus, my soul rests in You.

Pressing In

My calling is to press my face into the shoulder blades
of Jesus so that wherever He leads, I will go.
Margaret Feinberg

*H*old on tight and don't let go. That's the picture Margaret
Feinberg creates when she describes her calling as pressing
her face into the shoulder blades of Jesus. When we hold on
that tight, we show trust, we draw comfort, we give love.

When you hold onto Jesus like this, you draw in His scent
of strength and purpose. You feel the radiant warmth of His
love. And you're so intoxicated by it that you follow closely
so as not to lose a single precious moment basking in His
nearness. As you lean into Him, the direction of your steps
becomes almost irrelevant. Each cobblestone you traverse,
each ditch you leap across, becomes a victory. You care less
about where you're going and more about simply trusting
where He's leading you.

Press in. Inhale deeply. And don't lag.

Read Psalm 73:23–26.

Lord, make me so enamored of Your presence
that I press in for more.

Amazing Grace

Nothing seems more miraculous, more difficult
for us who insist on figuring things out,
than this matter of grace.
Elisabeth Elliot

John Newton, author of the hymn "Amazing Grace," said he had a habit of swearing that was as deeply rooted as a second nature. His last will and testament reads, "I was an apostate, a blasphemer, and an infidel." The former slave trader continued, "I was capable of anything; I had not the least fear of God before my eyes."

Yet God saved him. Why would God pour out His grace on such a violent man?

Because God loved him.

God loves you. Not because of who you are, not because of anything you've done, but just because He is the God of amazing grace. Nothing you've done is so bad that you are beyond the reach of His grace.

You won't be able to figure it out; it doesn't make sense. It's nothing short of miraculous, this matter of grace.

And it's a gift, freely given to you.

Read Ephesians 2:8–9.

Lord, thank You for loving me, for showing me
Your amazing grace.

Big Problems, Big Answers

*Sometimes the greatest answers to prayer happen
when you have no place to go but God.*

Carol Cymbala

*B*ad report . . . dreams crushed . . . hope lost. As awful as those moments are, they're the perfect time for God to do His work.

The impossibility of a situation means nothing to God. He delights in bringing answers when all we see are obstacles. He does some of His best work when there is no money, no time, no hope, no way out.

Are you ready to give up? Have you done everything humanly possible to solve the problem, but still you see no answer? Is it too big for you to fix, too overwhelming to handle, too much to bear?

Fall on your knees before God. You have nowhere else to turn. And that's just the time when God says to you, "Relax, My daughter. It isn't over until *I* say it's over." Big problems require big answers. And that's God's specialty.

Read Mark 10:27.

My problem is too big for me, Lord. I need a big answer.

Good for Evil

It is far better to endure patiently a smart which nobody feels
but yourself, than to commit a hasty action whose evil
consequences will extend to all connected with you;
and besides, the Bible bids us to return good for evil.

Charlotte Bronte

*G*od's way is often topsy-turvy to what we see. He promises that He works all things (even the bad) for our good. He promises to be our defender and the judge of anyone who shows us injustice. With these promises in place, He also gives us strength to endure pain when we have no way to escape it. He even enables us to return good for evil to those who hurt us.

That's exactly what we should do. Charlotte Bronte advises that it is better to endure a hurt patiently than to commit a hasty action that will cause evil consequences for everyone around. It's better that we hurt a little ourselves than we spread the hurt to others. And, beyond that, it's better to return good for evil.

Not easy; not comfortable; maybe not even fair. But God honoring.

And that's what matters.

Read Genesis 50:14–21.

Father, I thank You that You can turn evil into good.
Help me to trust You.

Opportune Interruptions

The telephone rings—loud, jarring . . .
dissolving my precious moment of stolen solitude.
Then . . . I suddenly know . . . that God
is in the ringing, that God is the interruption.

Edwina Gateley

"Stolen solitude." How true it is that to find precious moments to talk with God, we must steal the time from other tasks that beckon us. And even then, we cannot always get away. Interruptions dissolve those quiet moments, and the silence is shattered.

Like a broken dish, the fragility of silence is hard to repair. Instead, we usually set aside the pieces of what could have been and return to the world of ringing phones and demanding obligations.

But what if God's message is in the interruption? To see it that way changes everything. Instead of being unhappy or frustrated, seeing interruptions as God-given allows us to take God with us back into the demands of our day.

God speaks in many ways. We crave solitude—and we do need it at times. But when interruptions come, let God redeem them. He has a message for you.

Read Psalm 34:1.

. . . .

Lord, help me see You and hear You
in all the interruptions of my life.

Sharing the Path

We need someone to show us that our pain
can be redeemed and there is light ahead of us.
And the ones who show this best
are those who have lived deeply
and have not sidestepped suffering.
Rebecca Manley Pippert

She had buried her teen son ten months earlier and was deeply depressed. "The pain of losing a child is crushing," she said. "It grows more suffocating with each passing day he's not here."

An acquaintance introduced her to a couple who'd lost their son a few years earlier. They built a friendship that allowed them to grieve their losses together. The couple's transparency about the challenges of their journey offered her a bit of light for the dark, difficult path she was walking.

The path of pain is stony and rough. We want to know that our journey is worth something and that we will find light ahead. Sometimes it takes others who have walked the path to show us the way. And sometimes we will be the ones walking with others in pain. This is the body of Christ.

Read 2 Samuel 22:31–37.
. . . .

Lord, who in my life needs light for their path today?

He Hurts with Us

The only way in which Satan can persecute
or afflict God is through attacking the people of God.
The only way we can have personal victory
in the midst of these flying arrows . . .
is to call upon the Lord for help.
Edith Schaeffer

Remember when you were little and fell and scraped your knee? You didn't need to be coaxed to seek out a parent. You ran to your mom or dad like a shot, desperately wanting him or her to make it all better. Back then you couldn't understand how much your parent hurt when you were hurting.

On a more infinite scale, our heavenly Father hurts when we hurt. As Edith Schaeffer explains, this is the enemy's only ammunition against an indestructible God. He attacks God by attacking God's followers—us. But that ammunition proves ineffective if we call upon the Lord for help. Satan may persecute and afflict, he may send his arrows, but we are assured the victory. The Lord knows. He hurts with us. When our knees are scraped up by life, we can run to our Father. He promises to make it all better.

Read Psalm 91.

* * * * * * * * * * * * * * * * * * * *

Father, I'm in pain. Help me, Lord. Be merciful to me.

Getting Chaos under Control

God is a God of order.
We can tell that by looking at the universe.
None of it is random or accidental.
He doesn't want our lives to be either.

Stormie Omartian

As we go through our days at a breakneck pace, meeting each demand as it arises, we can easily become frazzled and frustrated. We put out one fire, only to find that three more have sparked into existence. Grabbing and aiming the fire extinguisher may keep life from erupting into an inferno, but God has a better way. He wants our lives to be orderly and intentional. We might have to say no to an activity we'd love to do, or we might have to disappoint people. But as we follow the Lord's model, we will become more productive and effective.

Living in an orderly way pleases God more than striving to get more done. Just as peace seems to emanate from the starry sky (a sky that was perfectly designed), trusting God to help plan our lives will replace sparks of chaos with a pleasant and warm glow.

Read Psalm 8:3–5.

. . . .

Father, teach me to live intentionally. Assure me that You
will take care of what I don't accomplish.

Around the Block

*Labor, therefore, to increase the fire of your desire,
and let not a moment pass without crying to Me
with humble voice, or without continual prayers
before Me for your neighbors.*

Catherine of Siena

The sixty-year-old woman is a familiar sight in her neighborhood. Even during long, cold Midwestern winters, she walks the same route every day. During her walk, she prays for salvation and spiritual growth for each household she passes, even if she hasn't met the family. She's seen God answer her prayers in surprising ways in the lives of the neighbors she does know. As a result, she expresses confidence that God is at work in the lives of those she has yet to meet.

Her intercession has had an impact on her own spiritual journey: "The longer I pray, the more I sense the depths of God's love for me, and for those around me." She understands Catherine's passion—the power of continual prayers for one's neighbors.

Your prayer time today is an opportunity to "increase the fire of your desire" and to bring those around you before your heavenly Father.

Read Ephesians 6:18.

*Lord, I ask that those around me will experience
and respond to Your great love today.*

God's Friend

The capacity to discern and do the will of God arises
out of friendship with God, cultivated through prayer,
times of quiet listening, and alert awareness.

Ruth Haley Barton

*C*lose friends know each other's secrets. They know what brings laughter. They can anticipate one another's reactions and read each others' hearts. Spending time together bonds the friendship. If one person doesn't take time to nurture the friendship, the pair drifts apart.

God knows all our secrets, all our hurts, and all our concerns. He knows when we will laugh and cry. He waits for us to meet with Him. God tells us if we seek Him, we'll find Him. When we search to know Him from Scripture and spend "friendship time" with God, we discover His ways. Our prayers are our side of the conversation. His leadings and promptings become clearer as we spend more time with Him.

As with any dear friendship, choose to set aside time to be with God, your best friend. He's waiting. He has so much He wants to share with you!

Read Exodus 33:11.

Dear Friend, I'm here. I want to spend time with You.

Worth the Wait

*At its best, our age is an age of searchers and discoverers,
and at its worst, an age that has domesticated
despair and learned to live with it happily.*

Flannery O'Connor

Waiting. Filling time while we wait for the phone to ring and deliver the news, whether good or bad. Standing in line. Preparing for an event. Or simply waiting "until things get better."

But what if the good news never comes? What if things don't get better? What if the waiting is meaningless? Too many people abandon hope, abandon trust, and decide, despite the contradiction, to live happily with their despair.

Christ has something far better in mind. In Him, we find meaning in the waiting. While we watch our hopes fade, He is turning our eyes toward a truer hope. While He makes us wait, we learn to trust our future dreams to Him. Waiting is hard, but waiting on God means the wait will be worth it.

Read Jeremiah 29:11.

Father, help me trust You while I'm in life's waiting room.

The Power of Praise

*God allows us to have disappointments, frustrations,
or even worse, because He wants us to see that our joy
is not in such worldly pleasures . . . our joy is in the fact
that we have a relationship with God.*

Catherine Marshall

God alone holds the "big picture" of our existence. He alone can lift us up to transcend anxieties and problems. Ah! What a gift to have such help!

Many people wonder why, if they stay close to God, they still experience disappointments, frustrations, or worse. They want God to insulate them from the realities of life. *If God loves me,* they think, *then these things shouldn't happen.*

But God allows those bad things in life. As Catherine Marshall explains, "He wants us to see that our joy is not in such worldly pleasures." Instead, our joy should be found simply in our relationship with God, not in what He does for us.

Step out of your difficulties for a moment. Look into the face of your heavenly Father who loves you so much. His love for you is all that really matters.

Read Habakkuk 3:17–19.

Thank You for loving me, Lord. My joy is in You alone.

Stand and Worship

Our worship is based on truth, not emotion;
it is based not on the fervency of our words,
but on the faithfulness of our God.
Emotion follows truth!

Kay Arthur

Through the truth-flowing words of our songs, we worship our Lord. We center our attention on Him and open our hearts. We read Scripture and reflect on His attributes and faithfulness through the generations. Tears flow; we fall to our knees in humility. Words may come easily or not at all.

Our worship is based on the truth of who God is. He is worthy of every word of praise, every tear of thanks, every smile of joy. It is not the fervency of our words or emotions that make for truth; the truth already exists. Worship is simply our way of responding to God's love and faithfulness.

Emotions are evidence of your deep devotion to God. Listen for His still, small voice or His gentle touch on your heart. Soak in the wonder of God's love. Linger in worship until you are full to overflowing. Praise Him. Thank Him. He deserves it.

Read John 4:24.

Lord, I worship You because of who You are!

Failing through Success

*For most of us, the subtle encroachment of pride
is more dangerous, and more likely to render us useless
to God and others, than any other kind of failure.*

Nancy DeMoss Wolgemuth

*F*ailure is a sad word. We fear failure. We don't want to fail at anything. Yet how do we view success? God doesn't measure success by the amount in our bank account, the rung we've reached on the corporate ladder, or even the number of our friends on Facebook. Sometimes it seems that His measures are upside down to ours. He treasures humility and hates pride.

Why? Because pride is dangerous. Nancy DeMoss Wolgemuth warns that it can render us useless, both to God and to others. How horrible to have great gifts and to be useless to God because of pride. But it happens slowly, subtly, almost without our noticing. We think a bit too highly of ourselves. We forge ahead without God's guidance. We do good things without the humility of trust in God.

Do you want to succeed in God's eyes? To be useful to Him? Serve with humility and love.

Read Proverbs 11:2.

. . . .

*Father, I want to be useful for You.
Keep me from the subtle hold of pride.*

The Small Stuff

What we call mundane is, in some very important ways,
significant in God's school of preparation.
Lysa TerKeurst

Mundane. Boring. Unspectacular. Unnoticed.

We want to do big things for God; the mundane is, well, mundane. But God says, "Right now, I've got tasks for you. Clean the church's toilets every week until I tell you to stop, and don't tell anyone what you're doing. See that single mom over there? Take her a home-cooked meal at least once a month, and don't tell others you're doing it. Mentor the worst hellion in the youth group. *Then* we'll talk about the next step."

Why does God make us prove ourselves in the small, unseen, everyday things before trusting us with more responsibility? Because integrity and character are born in the mundane, *ordinary* places where no one sees but God.

God cares more about who you are than about what you do. The mundane tasks you do today are significant—both in how they serve others and in how God is preparing you.

Read Matthew 6:1–4.

Thank You for trusting me with these mundane tasks, Lord.
Help me do them well.

Give It Away

*Because Jesus, the Gift, lives in the Christian,
the gifts and fruits are present in our lives.
They can radiate through us to a needy world.*

Leanne Payne

Gifts are meant to be given. We love handing a specially chosen gift to a friend, knowing she will be thrilled to open it. We give because we love. It would make no sense to purchase a gift, wrap it in beautiful paper, tie a shiny ribbon around it—and then put it on the top shelf of our closet. That brings no joy. The joy comes in the sharing, the giving.

Jesus was God's ultimate Gift to us, sent to our needy world so that His Spirit could radiate through us. The gifts (1 Corinthians 12:1–7) and fruit (Galatians 5:22–23) of the Spirit are given to us for the blessing and benefit of those around us. The gifts are meant to be given. We find no joy in keeping for ourselves what God has given us.

Give your gifts away. A needy world is waiting.

Read 1 Peter 4:8–11.

. . . .

*Please radiate through me to the needy world
around me, dear Jesus.*

He Won't Waste the Pain

Sometimes in life, we face incredibly complex situations—
some created by our fools, some by our own lack of wisdom.
All are allowed by God for a greater purpose in our lives.

Jan Silvious

*G*od is green. He lets no event go to waste in our lives. Whether it was a bad decision, a foolish action, or someone else's bad choice, incredibly complex situations can arise that leave us wondering how we can ever recover. But in God's economy, nothing is ever wasted—not even the bad stuff. Even if we got ourselves into the mess, God's grace prevails. As we live with the consequences of choices made, God watches over us, willingly transforming the situation for a greater purpose in our lives.

So take heart, dear sister. Whatever complex situation is making your life difficult, be encouraged. God has not given up on you; don't give up on yourself. He has a greater purpose in and through this situation. You may not be able to see it yet, but trust the promise. God won't waste the pain.

Read Psalm 30:5–12.

. . . .

Lord, I trust that You will turn this situation
around for Your glory.

Trials and Pleasures

"This earthly life is a battle," said Ma. "If it isn't one thing
to contend with, it's another. . . . The sooner you
make up your mind to that, the better off you are,
and the more thankful for your pleasures."

Laura Ingalls Wilder

God has given us many good things to enjoy, and yet this
world is cursed as the result of sin. Both parts of that equa-
tion remain true for our entire lives. If we expect "happily ever
after" in this world, we'll be disappointed. On the other hand,
if we look only at the bad things of life, our joy and gratitude
can be stifled.

Life is full of suffering, sorrow, betrayals, financial
hardships, and everyday trials. Even the best moments carry
hints of imperfection, and they end all too soon. But God
truly does bring good out of bad. He uses suffering to teach
us His sustaining power; He uses storms to bring rainbows.
We can take Ma's advice and refuse to be surprised when we
contend with difficulty. Once we make up our minds to do
that, we'll be so much more thankful for the pleasures God
has given.

Read 1 Peter 1:3–7.

* * * * * * * * * * * * * * * * * * *

Father, I thank You that You are good
even when circumstances aren't.

Longing for Home

*As we cope with the real world, it helps to keep
an eternal perspective, not one that can see
no further than today's pain.*

Barbara Johnson

It's hard, sometimes, to keep an eternal perspective, isn't it?
It's difficult to see past today's pain. Grief can be overwhelming. Sorrow can be devastating. Difficulties can seem insurmountable. If this life is all there is, then we would have little reason to hope.

Barbara Johnson challenges us to keep an eternal perspective, a focus on the promises of God for our forever home. We don't know exactly what it will look like, how it will feel, what we will do, but it's enough to know that God promises a place with no more death or mourning or crying or pain. Eternity in heaven with Him will be more wonderful than our minds can even begin to imagine.

As we struggle here on earth, it helps to remember we won't be staying long. We're just passing through. We're on our way home.

Read 2 Corinthians 4:16–18.

. . . .

*Lord God, please open my eyes to wonderful realities
of my heavenly home.*

Light in the Darkness

Like waifs clustered around a blazing fire,
we gathered around [the Bible], holding out our hearts
to its warmth and light. The blacker the night
around us grew, the brighter and truer . . .
burned the Word of God.

Corrie ten Boom

Corrie ten Boom gives witness to the power of the Word inside a Nazi concentration camp. In the midst of overwhelming horror, she read aloud from a smuggled Bible to the other women huddled in the barracks—their only home. They clustered around her to hear the reassuring words of hope in a place that teemed with hopelessness. And the Word stirred up a blazing hope and the fire of God's certain presence.

At this very moment, God is waiting to speak to you too. He reveals His great love for you in the Bible. When life's circumstances seem black, do not despair. In the pages of the Holy Book, God holds out light and warmth like a blazing fire. Let the Word of God warm you, guide you, and bring you light in the darkness.

Read Isaiah 42:16.

. . . .

Let Your precious Word bring me light
and warmth today, Lord.

Wrestling with God

After a person encounters God, she should be changed.
It is not enough for us to talk about
what we have experienced.
We should be living it out flamboyantly.

Priscilla Shirer

*T*alk is cheap. Experiences make for nice stories, but true change comes from an encounter that touches the heart and erupts into freedom.

We can't have a real encounter with God and walk away unscathed. This isn't goose bumps and gold dust. This is going toe-to-toe with God and wrestling out our questions, discussing our hurt feelings, and dealing with unforgiveness, pride, jealousy, addictions, or other besetting problems. Our heavenly Father loves us enough to confront us. He tells us the truth in love. We listen. We think. We challenge. We learn. We experience the only One who can change us from the inside out.

Such an encounter is more than just a good story to tell; it must cause you to live differently, to live in flamboyant joy! You are loved, so live like it!

Read Genesis 32:24–30.

. . . .

Lord, I want a real encounter with You.
I want to be transformed.

True Religion

I don't know anything about politics,
but I can read my Bible; and there I see that I must
feed the hungry, clothe the naked, and comfort the desolate;
and that Bible, I mean to follow.

Harriet Beecher Stowe

Sometimes the simplest truths are the most important. Caring for others is a great theme throughout Scripture. It doesn't take much research to understand that God calls on us—His hands and feet here on this planet—to take care of those in need. And need comes in a variety of colors. Maybe it's hunger. Maybe it's a lack of clothing or shelter. Maybe it's a need for financial assistance. Maybe it's just a shoulder to cry on or a few words of comfort.

Jesus said that unbelievers will know we are Christians by our love. His ministry was largely known for the way He treated the outcasts—touching and healing lepers, teaching women, accepting repentant sinners.

If we mean to follow our Bibles, then we mean to reach out to those in need in whatever way we can. It means touching, caring, giving, sharing, loving. After all, Jesus set the example.

Read Matthew 25:31–40.

Father, help me care for those in need as Jesus did.

Live to the Fullest

*Each person has a spiritual obligation before God
to learn how to live well, to live fully, as opposed
to knowing only how to live comfortably.*

Luci Swindoll

*A*h, comfort. Who doesn't want to live a comfortable life? We yearn for moments when we can wrap ourselves in a soft comforter, grasp a mug of hot tea in our hands, and listen to the warm crackling of a fire in the fireplace. Or maybe your picture of comfort includes exotic climes and a hammock stretched between tall palm trees.

When God provides such times of comfort, we can thank Him for that gift. But when days come that are far from comfortable, we can also take comfort in the fact that God is teaching us to live well, to live fully. He has more for us in life than just to live comfortably. He may call us to take uncomfortable risks or forego some of what is good in order to have what is best. Above all, it means having Jesus, who came to give us life to the fullest.

Read John 10:10.

. . . .

*Show me Your definition of life "to the full," Lord.
Help me live Your way.*

Giving Grace

*Pray for your enemies—even if you
have to do it with gritted teeth.*

Michelle Medlock Adams

Harsh words hit us like a fist. Our mouths fall open in disbelief when people take advantage of us, cheat us, make us feel like a punching bag. We can't imagine how such people can look at themselves in the mirror. But we *can* imagine how we'd like to get our own brand of justice.

What do we do with the hurt? The answer, as always, is to take it to Jesus. We turn over to Him what we cannot understand. We ask Him to give us grace to pray for those who hurt us—our enemies—for it may be true that those who inflict such pain have experienced deep hurts themselves. Maybe God wants to reach that person through us. Maybe our loving reaction will help soften a hardened heart.

But first, pray, gritted teeth and all. God will give you the grace you need.

Read Matthew 5:44–47.

. . . .

Lord, help me to be gracious when I have been wronged.

Second Chances

Every believer needs second chances.
Some of us need lots of them.

Beth Moore

Second chances. We all want them, but in the reality of this harsh world, second chances don't come easy. When unkind words are spoken in anger once too often, friendships are ruined. When trust is broken over and over, marriages are shattered. The end comes. We don't want to be hurt again. No more second chances.

But not so with God.

God sees your heart; He understands your weaknesses; He knows that you fail. You need second chances because you are not perfect. But God who is perfect sees the real you, and by His grace and mercy, He provides the second chance that the world wouldn't. It's in His unfailing love that God offers His outstretched hand to those who humble themselves, knowing they can't do it alone.

God offers lots of second chances. Take them. Don't give up, for He doesn't give up on you.

Read John 21:15–17.

* * * * * * * * * * * * * * * * * * *

Lord, I have failed many times but, in Your love,
I want to keep trying.

Complete Surrender

It is a great truth, wonderful as it is undeniable,
that all our happiness—temporal, spiritual, and eternal—
consists in one thing; namely, in resigning ourselves to God,
and in leaving ourselves with Him.

Madame Guyon

An infant has no choice in the matter of surrender. The loving parent lifts the child and carries her, providing what's best. We, too, should submit—to the Father's outstretched arms—but we *can* choose.

How foolish to resist His care, to insist on living apart from Him. With a love deep beyond our imagining, God wants only the best for His children. Thus, giving ourselves to Him brings true happiness. Choosing an alternate way would be foolish indeed. But often our will and actions move that direction, seeking what we feel we deserve, what makes us feel good. "Resigning" ourselves to Him means admitting that He sees the bigger picture and can be trusted.

Your heavenly Father loves you totally and completely. He wants to give you deep, abiding joy that is full and overflowing and lasting. Let Him enfold you and carry you in His loving arms.

Read Psalm 62:1–2.

· · · · · · · · · · · · · · · · · · · ·

I give myself to You today, Father. I rest in You.

Trading Up

*The most important exchange of all takes place
when God takes our guilt and replaces it
with His forgiveness, His cleansing.*

Evelyn Christenson

As children, we learn about trading: a peanut butter sandwich for tuna or a better spot in line at recess for a saved seat on the bus. This important skill helps us as we grow up and begin making purchases or considering career changes. The rule of thumb: always *trade up*. Let go of one thing for something of greater value to you. In a fair trade, each person is happy with the result.

When we trade the guilt and shame of past mistakes for forgiveness, everyone wins. We feel cleansed, set free, joyful. At the same time, God delights in our willingness to give up the burden He wants to carry for us anyway. His Son died to make it possible. He wants us to trade up!

While it may seem that we get the better end of this deal, the Lord is very pleased with the exchange.

Read 2 Corinthians 5:21.

*Lord, I willingly offer my burden of guilt to You
in exchange for Your sweet forgiveness.*

Fleeting Moments

For we have this moment to hold in our hands
and to touch as it slips through our fingers like sand;
yesterday's gone, and tomorrow may never come,
but we have this moment—today!

Gloria Gaither

You are holding a moment in your hands. What does it feel like? Is it a soft, silky rose—a moment to be cherished and enjoyed? Or is it a scruffy, scratchy shrub—an uncomfortable moment, one you'd like to forget? No matter how it feels, it will soon be gone like sand through your fingers. Time moves on. Time slips by.

Yesterday, you cannot change. The future, you cannot guarantee. Today, you have. Embrace it. Cup your hands around it. Look for the blessing in it, the hope in it, the joy in it. Focus on God and serve others even as the grains of time run through your fingers to be scattered in the wind. He longs for you to offer this moment back to Him, even as it slips away.

Today is yours. What will you do with this moment in your hands?

Read James 4:13–17.

. . . .

In today's hours and minutes, Lord, help me
look to You and cherish the moments.

Captive Hearts

I knew that I had a choice. I could give in
to my resentment . . . or I could choose
to believe what God's Word says to be true,
whether I felt it was or not.

Gracia Burnham

When Gracia Burnham penned these words, she didn't mean them lightly. She had been held captive in a jungle by terrorists for over a year. On the brink of starvation, without modern conveniences, stripped of all freedom and privacy, she recognized that she was held doubly captive—physically and emotionally—if she allowed herself to become angry and to resent her captors. She chose to trust God, knowing that even this horrible circumstance was in His good and perfect plan for her life. She chose to let God work in her and refused to put up walls of bitterness.

What is it, beloved, that is causing you hurt, bitterness, resentment? You have a choice. You can give in to those feelings or, like Gracia, you can choose to believe that what God's Word says is true, whether it feels like it or not.

One choice leads to captivity, the other to freedom.

Read John 17:13–17.

God, help me to give up my resentment and bitterness.
I want to be free.

Trouble in This World

He said not, "Thou shalt not be tempested,
thou shalt not be travailed, thou shalt not be diseased";
but he said, "Thou shalt not be overcome."

Julian of Norwich

God never promised to make life easy. Julian of Norwich understood that God never said that His followers would be excused from the storms of life or the travail of difficulties or the sorrows of disease and discomfort. But God *did* say that we would not be overcome.

Many people want it to be different. They don't want to believe in a God who would allow storms and sorrows and suffering. Yet God is preparing a perfect place for His followers—it's called heaven. For now, however, we are in the world—called to trust no matter what, called to stand strong. We have the word of the One who has overcome, the One who makes all things right, the One who has the power to bring good from evil.

Take your tempests and trials to the One who has overcome the world. He will take care of you.

Read John 16:33.

. . . .

Heavenly Father, when I'm overwhelmed,
it's a blessing to know that I'm not overcome.

Defining Moments

Crisis has happened. What will come of this? . . .
We have a choice to be conformed to the ordinary,
the expected, the easier path.
Or we can choose to let this event transform us.

Miriam Neff

When tragedy strikes, the pain can knock us off our feet. We face the tempestuous emotions of anger, denial, grief, and even depression. We fear for the future, wondering what can possibly come of this situation. What good can God bring from this crisis?

In those moments, we have a choice. We can choose the path that lets our emotions take over; the path that leads us into resentment and bitterness. Or we can choose the less expected path of allowing ourselves to be transformed by God. We can choose to let Him work in us to do His will. When the world sees an out-of-the-ordinary response to crises in life, it sits up and takes notice.

You can come out of the crisis on the other side—stronger and more dependent on God. He doesn't want tragedies to destroy you or define you. He wants to transform you.

It's your choice.

Read James 1:2–4.

. . . .

Lord, please don't let this crisis be wasted on me.
I want to be transformed.

True Peace

*It was kind of like a cave-in—this great big peace
just kind of dumped in on me, washed in on me
like a wave. . . . "It's God," I said.*

Jan Karon

We long for peace. A few moments of quiet when the world doesn't intrude in our thoughts. A respite from battles with folks who hurt us or disagree with us. We'd even like to see world peace. We want something that goes deep, that lasts, that penetrates our very souls.

Jesus brings that kind of peace. When we find Jesus, we find peace that passes understanding, peace that does not go away, peace that gives rest to our fears and our troubled hearts. Jesus's kind of peace dumps on us like a cave-in, washes over us like a wave—inescapable, strong, overwhelming. His peace doesn't change or disappear.

What are you facing today? Is your world less than peaceful? Jesus promises peace; it's a gift He'll freely give you. Let it dump on you, overwhelm you, and wash over you. Today, walk in peace.

Read John 14:26–27.

. . . .

*Father, I thank You for the presence and guidance
of Your Holy Spirit.*

Bread of Life

When we view God as just a source of information . . .
we forget that God's words are not merely words,
but life to be ingested.

Margaret Feinberg

*F*or what do you hunger? What do you need to fill and fulfill you? Maybe you're not sure what's causing those pangs of emptiness and, therefore, nothing satisfies.

Consider your approach to God's Word. Are you reading because it's on your to-do list? Do you want to learn more about God? Are you seeking His will? If spending time in the Word leaves you feeling empty, perhaps it's time to put aside merely reading for head knowledge in exchange for fully engaging your heart.

To ingest the Word means to consume it and to let it fill the void, empty places. Read God's Word not just for information but as life-giving words that sustain you and become a part of you. Crave His every word, ingest it, be satisfied by it, and let it nourish your soul and your life.

Read John 6:26–35.

Put a craving in me, Lord, that is only satisfied
by ingesting Your Word.

Your Hands, Your Feet

God lays down certain physical laws.
Yet we seem to be continually expecting that
He will work a miracle—i.e. break His own laws
expressly to relieve us of responsibility.

Florence Nightingale

You sit bedside with an ailing friend. You hug a neighbor receiving tragic news. You agonize over a child living with sin's consequences. *They don't deserve this*, you think. *Why can't God relieve the torturous pain?* As Florence Nightingale reminds us, God lays down certain physical laws. In some cases, He will break through with a miracle. At other times, He does not. The desire to see a miracle must not merely reflect a desire to be relieved of responsibility.

What is that responsibility? Perhaps it is to pray fervently. Perhaps it is to maintain an unwavering faith that witnesses to others. Perhaps it is to seek God's approval as reward enough. Nobody knows the bigger picture or the thoughts of God. Whatever He chooses to do, He needs you, for you are His hands and feet in the world.

Your touch, your words, your prayers bring Him into your hurting world.

Read James 2:15–17.

. . . .

Take my words, my hands, my feet into Your world today, Lord.

Choose Contentment

Oh what a happy soul I am, although I cannot see,
I am resolved that in this world, contented I will be.
How many blessings I enjoy that other people don't!
To weep and sigh because I'm blind I cannot and I won't.

Fanny Crosby

We must resolve to be content; it is an act of our will. Contentment is a choice, not a result of a job completed or of perfect life circumstances. If we connect contentment to a work or expectation, then contentment will only come to those who finish the job. If we connect contentment with perfect life circumstances, well—we will probably never find it.

Life is filled with unfinished and interrupted work, yet contentment is available. Or, as with Fanny Crosby, life may deal us difficult circumstances beyond our control. We can weep and sigh, or we can decide that we cannot and won't do so. Instead we can choose to focus on the blessings we enjoy.

Choose today to find contentment, to focus on the blessings in your life. Grab those blessings and don't let go. Focus on thankfulness and, like Fanny, you will find true contentment.

Read Philippians 4:11–13.

Jesus, I choose today to focus on the blessings
You have so generously given me.

Calvary's Love

*If I take offence easily; if I am content to continue
in cold unfriendliness, though friendship be possible,
then I know nothing of Calvary's love.*

Amy Carmichael

Our feelings get hurt easily when we forget about God's big love for us. When others' sins and offenses become our focus, we have lost our correct focus as believers. As daughters of God, our attention is to be on Him and what He has done for us, not on others and how they hurt us. We must remember that when we did not deserve it, Christ chose not only to forgive us of all our sin but also to declare us righteous.

Amy Carmichael points out that we know nothing of Calvary's love if we accept the forgiveness of Christ but then refuse to forgive others. When our cups are full of Christ's forgiveness, we are able to spill that grace onto the people in our lives. As we become full of God's great grace for us, we can overflow with unconditional love for others.

Read Ephesians 4:32.

*Lord, keep my eyes on You and what You have done,
not on others and what they have done to me.*

The Hard Work of Love

*If you do the works of love before the emotions match up,
the feelings of love will eventually follow along.*

Jill Briscoe

*M*ovies make love look easy—romance is something you "fall into." But real love often involves more of a commitment than a good feeling. Sometimes we have to *do* love even when we don't *feel* love.

At times it's just plain hard to love. Those closest to us can hurt us the most. We don't *feel* like loving the husband who is acting insensitive, the child who is being rebellious, the parent who is overbearing, or the friend who is demanding. We can even justify why we shouldn't have to show them any love whatsoever!

But love is more than just a feeling; instead, it's a choice. We do the works of love and let the emotions catch up later. As Jill Briscoe says, eventually the feelings will follow along. We may not always feel like loving, but God can give us the grace to love even the unlovely.

Read 1 Corinthians 13:1–7.

*God, help me to love in word and in works,
even when others are unlovely.*

Let Him Love You

*This wild God of mine . . . loves me . . . not in the way
we usually translate when we hear, "God loves us."
Which usually sounds like "because He has to" or meaning
"He tolerates you." No. He loves me as a Lover loves.*

Stasi Eldredge

*L*ove." The word speaks to the soul, the emotions, the
heart. A child cuddled by Mom or Dad. A toddler tod-
dling toward outstretched arms. Friends reunited with bear
hugs. An engaged couple walking hand in hand, then gazing
into each other's eyes. Newlyweds driving from the reception,
beginning life together.

Whatever feelings the word *love* evokes, multiply them by
thousands to gain a glimpse of God's love for you. God's love
goes beyond any kind of human love we can experience. It is
perfect love—He loves us not because He *has* to, not because
He *tolerates* us, but because He is wildly *in love* with us. Such
love is almost unimaginable—but it is true; it is real; it is yours.

Let that thought, that picture, those emotions wash over
you, cleansing you of any hesitancy or fear in your relationship
with Him. He loves you as a *lover* loves.

Read Ephesians 3:14–19.
. . . .

Thank You, God, for loving me so much.

Heavenly Embrace

*Could I have been in heaven without the love of God,
it would have been a hell to me; for, in truth,
it is the absence and presence of God
that makes heaven or hell.*

Anne Bradstreet

What is heaven anyway? We know that the images of sitting on clouds playing the harp all day aren't true, but what *is* true? Heaven is a perfect place, yes, but there has to be more. There must be more than streets of gold and pearly gates to make it so appealing.

What Anne Bradstreet longed for over three hundred years ago is exactly what we desire as well: a relationship. Being near the One who loves us more than life itself. Finally meeting the God who was willing to sacrifice His own Son so that we could be with Him. Being looked at by Someone who knows how imperfect we are, how often we've messed up, yet still sees us as beautiful and loves us with an everlasting love.

That's heaven. Seeing your Savior, your Lover, your Friend—and being held in His embrace forever.

Read 1 Thessalonians 4:16–17.

. . . .

*Father God, I want to be near You.
I look forward to being with You forever.*

Daughter of the King

If I am a princess in rags and tatters,
I can be a princess inside. . . . It is a great deal more
of a triumph to be one all the time when no one knows it.
Frances Hodgson Burnett

You are a daughter of the King. Perhaps it's hard to believe that. You buy some of your clothes at yard sales. Your "chariot" has quite a few miles on it. Your house doesn't look like a castle, and it needs remodeling. But you're in temporary quarters now. If Jesus is your Savior, then your Father is King of the whole universe—imagine it! And someday you will live with Him.

In the meantime, He calls you to be a princess *on the inside*. Sure, maybe it's a little more of a challenge, because no one sees, no one knows, no one necessarily expects you to act like the King's daughter. But that is the best triumph of all— to live like the princess you are when no one else knows, to live like Jesus even when it's not expected.

Live for your King, your Highness. You are His princess.

Read Matthew 5:3–10.

My King, thank You for calling me Your own daughter.
I love You.

The Best Gift

*God wants us to seek Him not merely
for the functions He performs but just
for the sheer joy of relationship with Him.*

Mary Demuth

*R*ecall your very favorite birthday present as a child. Maybe it was a special doll, a handmade sweater, or a favorite book or musical selection. While the gift may have been memorable, it's likely that your memory of the giver is even more poignant. Watching her face mirror yours as she saw your delighted expression, the awareness of how well she knew you in order to choose this particular gift, the generosity and sacrifice of buying or making this gift for you—they all said one thing: *I know you, and I love you.*

Our lives are brimming with lovely gifts from God. It's so important that we don't forget for a moment to seek to know and love the Giver more than the gifts. He alone is the best gift we could ever receive.

Smile with sheer joy! You have a relationship with the God who knows you best!

Read James 1:17.

. . . .

*Lord, I have sheer joy in the fact
that You know me and love me.*

To Know Love

Love and pain go together, for a time at least.
If you would know love, you must know pain too.
Hannah Hurnard

We were made for a perfect world, but we do not live in one. In this life, love and pain come paired; one does not exist without the other. For now, the consolations of love come tinged with grief, misunderstanding, and even loss.

Yet Hannah Hurnard describes pain as a pathway to understanding the kind of all-encompassing love God has for us. To get to the heights, we must go through the valley. To understand love, we must be willing to experience pain— for true love calls for giving, for sacrifice, for facing hurt and loss.

Jesus Himself showed the ultimate love by His willingness to sacrifice His life for us. His love for us was worth whatever pain it took to bring us to Himself. If we want to truly love, we must willingly follow His example.

Read 1 John 3:16.

. . . .

Help me to understand that pain teaches me
more about Your love, dear Lord.

Love Lasts

*Love is the only thing that we can carry
with us when we go, and it makes the end so easy.*
Louisa May Alcott

Can the pain of death really be eased? In *Little Women*, as Beth neared the end of her life, she knew that love would go with her; love would make her final days easier to bear.

We don't like to think about life's end. With sorrow, we grieve the loss of those who leave us through death. To contemplate our own passing is hardly a way we'd want to spend an afternoon.

Yet we must think about it. We must know both our eternal destiny and our duty to fulfill our God-appointed tasks in this life. Above all, we must love. Love those close to us with a love that looks past wrongs and hurts and endures anyway. Love those far away with a love that causes us to care, to serve, to give where we can.

Love will go with us into eternity. Love alone will last.

Read 1 Corinthians 13:13.
. . . .

Lord, help me to carry Your love with me wherever I go today.

The Workshop

What Christ asks of us is a roomy workshop,
for when He comes into the soul, He comes
as a craftsman and brings His tools with Him.

Evelyn Underhill

*J*esus wants to move into our souls. He needs a workshop, a place to lay out the tools He will use as He crafts His purposes in our lives. He needs room to do His work.

So we must clear out the clutter taking up space—the clutter of a desire for wealth and prestige, the accumulation of stuff, or a craving to be noticed and appreciated. Before we can give Christ His workshop, we must make space. Spiritual housecleaning is a process of letting go of these desires and freeing ourselves from worldly attachments.

Invite Jesus into the workshop of your life. You may need His help to clean it up, but He willingly does it. He is the Master Craftsman and He has a plan more beautiful than you can imagine. Stop in. Take a look. See what He's working on in you today.

Read 1 John 2:15–17.

. . . .

Holy Spirit, I give You room today to do Your work in me.

Just a Touch

Just as the hemorrhaging woman crept up behind Jesus,
so do we try to keep our "stuff" secret,
hoping no one will notice our spiritual anemia,
the eternal emotional bloodletting.

Jane Rubietta

She kept her head bowed low and clutched her scarf tightly around her head. She shuffled through the crowd. If anyone knew who she was and the illness she had, they'd be panic-stricken because she was touching everyone—not really able to help it in the crush of the crowd. She had been bleeding for twelve years, and this made her ritually unclean. No one should touch her; she should touch no one.

But her mission was worth the risk of detection. She had a plan. Jesus had come to town, Jesus the healer. She would simply get close enough to reach out and touch His robe, then receive His healing.

We keep our heads low to hide our pain. We put on a happy face. We want to remain undetected so that no one sees our "spiritual anemia."

Jesus invites you to come close. Just a touch will heal you.

Read Mark 5:25–32.

· ·

I don't want to hide anymore, Lord.
Please touch me and make me whole.

Finding the "Real Good"

Perfection is attained through the active and positive effort to wrench a real good out of a real evil.

Dorothy Sayers

How do we picture perfection? A scenic and restful holiday? A perfectly shaped body? A spotless home? Striving for perfection in those areas is nothing short of frustrating—there will always be someone with a more exotic holiday or a leaner body or a more finely decorated house. We are fighting a losing battle.

Dorothy Sayers has another take on perfection. She asks us to live our lives wrenching *real good* out of *real evil*, living as Jesus lived during His time on this planet. When our evil world threatens to close in, we live as light in the darkness, bringing hope and joy to those around us. We do not sugarcoat evil, but we put our trust in God, knowing that He alone can bring good from evil.

You will find God's brand of perfection as you bring light to your dark world.

Read Hebrews 10:14–17.

. . . .

Father, help me to bring light to my world today.

We've Only Just Begun

There is nothing sadder than an unfulfilled life. . . .
Dreams don't come with expiration dates.

Martha Bolton

Deep inside each of us, God has placed desires. We have gifts, talents, and dreams of what we want to do. Years pass. We continue to live our lives, but we keep looking for that fulfillment. At times, we find ourselves delayed or sidetracked by life's unexpected circumstances.

Maybe you don't feel like you're living your dream—but don't get discouraged. Dreams don't come with expiration dates. Taking a circuitous route to your dream doesn't mean you won't get there. Life's unexpected circumstances come as no surprise to God. Instead, you may find that God is moving you toward a dream perfected for you—better than you could have imagined. The life you live and the wisdom you gain will make the attainment of your dream that much sweeter. Maybe that will prove to be the purpose of the delay all along.

Be patient. God is not finished with you—or your dreams—yet.

Read Joshua 14:6–13.

Help me to see the possibilities and opportunities
You have for me, Lord.

One More Step

The last and foundational part of my perseverance
is born out of my faith. When all those other things . . .
run out or fall short, my faith is the thing that enables me
to just show up and take one more step.

Michelle Akers

It's tough to keep going. When our strength is gone, when that next step takes such tremendous effort, when our body screams in protest and our brain has called in sick—what will motivate us to keep moving forward? What reason will move our tired mind and limbs?

There's only one: Jesus. Perseverance is born out of faith in Him.

Everything else will run out. Our own determination, desires, or dreams may not be enough to keep us going. But faith in the One who calmed the raging sea, healed the sick, raised the dead, and gave sight to the blind—that will keep us showing up and taking one more step.

Whatever you've been called to do, know this: He will provide strength and energy for the work to do it. No matter how tired you are today, faith will help you persevere. Take that next step. Your faith will sustain you.

Read Isaiah 40:30–31.

. . . .

Lord, I'm tired. Give me strength to take
the next step and follow You.

First Meetings

Being alert to the possibility that God
may bring a person across our path will change
our attitude toward first meetings.

Dee Brestin

We have many first meetings. Some blossom into lifelong relationships; others last only a few minutes. But that first "hello" becomes important when we consider the possibility that God wants us to minister to that person, if for only a moment.

Haven't we all received a smile from a stranger just when we needed one? Or a helping hand? When we've been encouraged out of the blue in that way, we praise God for the unexpected blessing.

You never know whom you might meet today. Your smile may light up the day for a woman who is hurting. Your kind offer of help may rebuild someone's trust in the human race. And if you're dealing with sorrow, perhaps you'll meet someone who's been there, and she can have the joy of ministering to you.

Be alert to your first meetings today. See what surprises God has in store!

Read 2 Thessalonians 1:11.

* * * * * * * * * * * * * * * * * * *

Lord, help me to see my first meetings through Your eyes.

In God's Eyes

That's what God says when He looks upon you, dear one.
"Ta-da! I did it! She's perfect, she's finished,
and she's all Mine." You are gorgeous to God simply
because you're covered in the blood of His Son.

Liz Curtis Higgs

Do you hurry past the full-length mirror in the hallway? You know if you stop, you'll be disappointed. That reflection doesn't resemble the *you* inside. What you see doesn't seem to reflect what *is*. You move forward to look at the details, mainly wrinkles, and wonder if the product you saw on TV really would tighten up your eyes. You step back and admit that bikini days are over. The sequined dress in the back corner of your closet will probably never fit again. No one will be chasing you down for a photo for their magazine cover.

But you know what? God says you're just right. Age has made you a richer person inside, a wiser woman, a more compassionate woman, a stronger woman. Jesus has made you beautiful.

The magazine cover photos are always touched up, but you? You're gorgeous! So give that reflection a great big smile!

Read 1 John 1:7.

. . . .

Lord, help me see myself the way You do.
Thank You for making me just right!

Anchored in God

How shall we fix our eyes on things unseen?
There is no answer but faith, faith in the character
of God Himself. That and no other
is the anchor for our souls.

Elisabeth Elliot

The anchor of a great ship seems small compared to the vessel itself. Yet when dropped to the ocean floor, it holds even the largest vessel in place.

Faith in our God is the anchor of our souls, holding us safe. When questions don't have answers, faith knows that God does. When circumstances don't make sense, faith knows that God has the big picture. When we need something to hold us safely in the harbor when the storms come, faith knows that God will not fail us. Faith is trusting in the character of God Himself.

Gaze not on what life appears to be; instead, anchor your soul in who God is. He will hold you steady. No matter what is happening in your life today, have faith. God is still God—good, sovereign, omniscient, omnipotent, wise, faithful, and unchanging.

Read 2 Corinthians 5:7.

Anchor my soul today, God—in You.

I Will Obey

When God gives a command or a vision of truth,
it is never a question of what He will do,
but what we will do.

Henrietta Mears

God is doing great things all around us. He is opening doors and changing hearts. Like Aslan in Narnia, He is on the move—warming hearts toward Him, seeking the lost, bringing His loving touch to those who hurt. So the issue, as Henrietta Mears explains, is what *we* are going to do.

In other words, will we join Him? Are we willing to engage in His unseen plans? We can look at the world around us and get angry. We can be apathetic and decide the situation is hopeless. We can hunker down and avoid contact. Or . . . we can decide we will join God in His work, doing whatever He calls us to do to spread His truth in a needy world.

Are you in?

Read Matthew 4:19.

. . . .

Lord, I'm in. What can I do to serve You today?

True Home

The more homelike heaven becomes,
the more you feel like an alien or stranger on earth.
Joni Eareckson Tada

*H*ome. The word evokes thoughts of the place where you rest your head and satisfy your hunger. Home is a refuge from the craziness of life—everything you need is there. Best of all, home is where everyone knows you and loves you anyway.

For the Christian, heaven is home. It is the only place where you won't have any need. Everyone will know and love you, but even more reassuring, everyone will know and love the Lord. Earthly life is confusing, full of dilemmas, pitfalls, and unpleasant surprises. Life in our eternal, heavenly home will be a ceaseless series of certainties, with times of joy and praise that will fill us with everlasting peace.

It's no surprise we feel uneasy here, like aliens in a strange world. We were created to walk with God. Heaven is our true home.

Read John 17:11.

. . . .

I look forward to my true home with You in heaven, Lord.

He Is Calling

God calls them just the way they are,
then He empowers them to get their act together!
Beth Moore

God often touches our hearts to do something for Him, but we feel unsure of ourselves, inadequate, unqualified. Many women called by God may have felt that way as well, but they didn't make excuses:

Mary didn't say, "I'm too young."

Rahab didn't say, "I have a business to run."

Esther didn't say, "I could be killed!"

Deborah didn't say, "A woman judge?"

Phoebe didn't say, "I don't travel alone."

After the call, God equipped these women to do what He needed, but they first had to be willing.

He is calling you today for an important job, a job He knows you can do because, well, He's going to work through you.

He just needs you to say, "Yes, Lord!"

Read Isaiah 6:7–8.

. . . .

Yes, Lord. Show me what You want me to do.

Bring Your Heart

I cannot ask Thee to restore the years of canker
and of blight, for Thou hast called me o'er and o'er,
and sought me thro' the long, dark night;
I cannot ask it, Lord, but see I bring a broken heart to Thee!

Mary Artemisia Lathbury

*T*he years of canker and of blight." It's old language, but the words deeply resonate if we have spent many years living far from God, spending our lives in what will not last, seeking for a joy we could never find. Indeed, being far from Him is like living in a "long, dark night."

We may look back across years where we lived our own way and wish we could get them back. If only we had sought God sooner. If only we had heard that voice calling us "o'er and o'er." Then we could have saved ourselves much pain and heartache.

God will not turn back time, but He readily accepts broken hearts. He specializes in taking hearts beaten and bruised by life and healing them.

Come to Him with your broken heart, your fragmented soul, your worn baggage. He will make you whole.

Read Psalm 51:17.

* *

Lord, I come to You as I am. Make me Yours.

The Greatest Gift

It takes faith to come to God simply to be with Him.
It proves, first of all, that we believe He exists.
And that He is our greatest gift.

Stormie Omartian

Sometimes we get to the end of a long day and flop exhausted into the nearest chair, only to find ourselves asking, "What did I really accomplish today?" Maybe our accomplishments were many, but we found no joy in them. Or perhaps of all the tasks we did, nothing seemed very valuable or worthwhile in the grand scheme of things.

Stormie Omartian suggests an action that will put every other thing we do into its proper perspective: Come to God simply to be with Him.

In the fast pace of today's world with its focus on achievement and financial success, we may lose sight of our greatest treasure—our relationship with our loving God. The best way to grow more deeply in love with Him is to carve out time every day to be with Him.

Simply bask in His goodness. He is our greatest gift.

Read Psalm 31:19.

It's amazing—you want to spend time with me.
So here I am to worship You.

Walk in Truth

It is one thing to stand in truth, to believe it,
and to embrace it, yet, there's more than this in girding
our loins with truth; we are to walk in truth.

Kay Arthur

We long for truth. We appreciate the people in our lives who tell us the truth. Truth means we can count on it. Even if it's a difficult observation or statement, we at least have a foundation to work from to make a change.

As believers, we count on God's Word as truth. We stand on it, we believe it, we embrace it. But we must do one more thing—we must *walk* in it. What we do, what we say, how we live, the example we set, the attitudes we show—all must line up with the truth to which we have committed our lives.

It isn't always easy, but it's vital. We have found the truth that changes the world, changes lives, changes hearts. Let that truth affect every step you take, today and every day.

Read Psalm 86:11.

Lord, let my actions reveal my faith in Your Word as truth.

Strength to Go On

Giving unlocks our own hearts to God's comfort
and His new plans for our lives after tragedy
and grief have done their worst.

Eugenia Price

She used to volunteer regularly at her church's food pantry, but after the sudden death of her newborn son eight months earlier, she had retreated as she and her family mourned.

"I wondered if I would ever feel anything but sadness again in my life," she said. "But I felt a glimmer of joy when I returned to volunteer at the food pantry and placed some groceries in the arms of an elderly man. He smiled at me. I smiled back at him. It had been a long time since I'd smiled."

If tragedy and grief have done their worst, Eugenia Price would advise, then after your time of mourning, find ways to serve others. You may not feel like you have much to offer, but giving unlocks your heart to receive God's comfort. He will provide the strength to go on.

Read Psalm 119:50.

. . . .

Please strengthen me to serve another today,
O God of all comfort.

Be Still

*He sat for a long time and thought to himself
that he wished he knew how to pray, yet he knew,
untaught, how by abandonment of himself
to let the quietness take hold of him.*

Elizabeth Goudge

How can we let the quietness "take hold" of us? Our lives are so very busy. Finding time to be still, to be quiet, seems like an unattainable luxury.

But we must try. Days will pass and, if we wait until we have the time or the attitude or the setting to pray, we may never get around to it. We will wonder why we feel so harried and why God seems so far away. At that time, we must remember what we already know—that we must abandon ourselves and let the quiet take hold.

"Be still, and know that I am God," wrote the psalmist (Psalm 46:10). God invites us to, at least for a few moments, cease our physical and mental activity and simply bask in who He is. We don't need to *do* or *say* anything; we simply need to *be* with God.

Read Psalm 46:10.

*Here I am, gracious Father.
I just want to sit here quietly with You.*

True Friends

Your friendships are vital to your relationship with God.
Your friends are either pulling you down (away from God)
or pulling you along and/or up (toward God).

Elizabeth George

*E*ver think of your friendships as a vital part of your relationship with God? Those hearts knitted together with you and God are gifts from on high. Such friends pull us up toward God, always encouraging us to seek Him. We learn from one another's experiences. We're encouraged to break out of mediocrity and stretch into the persons we were created to be.

Some friends influence our dreams. Some mentor us. Some connect us to other important relationships. And our dearest friends would tear off the roof to set us before Jesus!

But friends can also pull us away from God if we let them. Some friendships can send us in wrong directions. We need to discern these and set them aside.

Thank God for good friends. Keep them close. Pray for them, care for them, love them. They are God's gift to you, for now and for eternity.

Read Mark 2:2–4.

Jesus, thank You for Your friendship.
Help me be a true friend to others.

We Win!

*We are not only striving toward victory
but fighting from the position of victory.*

Corrie ten Boom

If a soldier knew that no matter how hard he fought, his army was going to lose the war, he might drop his ammunition and desert. On the other hand, if word came down that victory was absolutely assured, he would fight on with renewed strength.

We are in a battle; make no mistake about it. Simply by being followers of Christ, we are archenemies of Satan. We are targets—and many of us face his attacks every day.

But guess what? Jesus has already told us the outcome of the war. We win!

Victory is assured in the war, but many battles remain to be fought in the meantime. As Corrie says, we are not just striving *for* victory; we are fighting *from the position* of victory. Every battle we win pushes back the darkness a little further. Every soul saved is another life rescued for God's kingdom.

Fight on.

Read 1 John 5:4.

I am ready for battle today, Lord. Thank You that we win!

Faith to Move Mountains

*Oh, for the mighty, convicting, convincing power
of the Holy Ghost! Oh, for faith to remove mountains,
to expect them to be removed!
Pray for us, for the mountains are very tangible,
and our faith is very weak.*

Amy Carmichael

As Amy Carmichael penned these words, she was on her way to Japan to serve as a missionary. Even she, now looked upon as a model for world missions, admitted that she struggled with trusting God. The mountains that stood in the way of sharing Christ were tangible and seemingly impassable. Her faith seemed too weak to move them. So she prayed for the Holy Spirit to fill her with the faith she needed.

Take comfort in that, dear sister. You don't need "perfect faith" in order for God to use you. You need only to be willing. When you feel weak, you can go to the Source who promises to give you the faith you need.

What mountains are on your horizon, threatening to block God's work? What challenge seems more than you can handle? Cry out to God. He will give you faith to move mountains.

Read Matthew 21:21–22.

. . . .

Lord, I do believe. Help me overcome my unbelief.

Knowing Truth

Satan isn't called the Father of Lies for nothing.
He opened his cozy chat with [Eve] using a deliberate lie—
misquoting God, even putting words in the Lord's mouth.

Liz Curtis Higgs

We don't like to be lied to, but sometimes we fall for lies in spite of ourselves. It all depends on what we're looking for. If we're desperate to look younger, we'll believe anything about the special cream sold on TV. If we want quick wealth, we'll fall for the online ad with all its impossible promises.

You see, Satan plays on our weaknesses. Just as he sensed that Eve wanted to know more about God and built his cozy chat with her around that very information, so he observes where we are most vulnerable. He's looking for ways to get us off track spiritually—he'll even sometimes quote God's Word—because he wants nothing more than to come between us and God. If we listen, we lose.

Our best defense is intimate knowledge of the truth found in God's Word. Read it. Study it. Talk about it. Understand it.

How will you know the truth? Open God's Word. He'll gladly reveal it.

Read Psalm 119:30.

. . . .

Help me, Father, to study Your Word so I know the truth.

World-Weary

I love neither the world, nor the things of the world;
nor do I believe that anything that does not come
from Thee can give me pleasure;
everything else seems to me a heavy cross.

Teresa of Avila

World-weariness isn't a twentieth-century phenomenon. Teresa of Avila faced it as she wrote these words in the sixteenth century. She was tired of chasing things that disappointed, tired of seeking satisfaction in that which ultimately fell flat. She describes these pursuits as a "heavy cross." Only that which came from the hand of God could give her true pleasure.

All around us, messages promising pleasure fill our senses. We are told to buy this, taste that, watch this, and we will be happy. Only when we learn to no longer love the world or the things of the world, only when we understand that seeking pleasure in these worldly pursuits is merely a heavy cross—only then will we begin to understand where true pleasure lies.

Your greatest joy, dear sister, is found in seeking after God and enjoying what He gives. Anything else will disappoint.

Read Isaiah 55:2–3.

Father, my greatest joy is found in seeking and finding You.

Beauty from Ashes

We must believe that God permits failure—
that a loving God permits hard things;
because the hard things bring the greatest victories,
the deepest lessons, the most lasting changes.

Carole Mayhall

*F*ailure. The thought of it causes our faces to turn red and our heads to drop in despair. We don't always understand why it is a part of life. We try to avoid it. Yet, despite our best efforts, it happens. Shame, disappointment, and humiliation hit us like tidal waves. People distance themselves from us. Ministry crumbles before our eyes.

But from the ashes of devastation, God can bring beauty. God permits hard things—yes, even failures—because He knows that through the failures come great victories, deep lessons, and lasting change.

God can bring beauty from the ashes of our failure, too, if we let Him, if we choose to believe He is still at work, if we trust Him enough.

Are you facing hard things today? Trust God for the victory, the lessons, the changes. He loves you. He wants to bring beauty from the ashes.

Read Isaiah 61:1–3.

. . . .

God, I trust You with my hard things today.
I know You can bring beauty from ashes.

Our Sacred Sculptor

If we are willing to be molded by His hands,
the Lord will shower us, our men, and our relationships
with abundance. That is the way He works.

Shaunti Feldhahn

When a potter picks up his clay, it's usually a stiff, cold, shapeless block. It takes patience and strong hands to soften the clay before it can be molded. During this time, the artist gets to delight in the process of creation and dream about his finished product.

Picture our heavenly Father, with His strong hands, desiring to shape you for His glory, for your benefit, and for others' blessing. How much patience will He need to make you pliable? How resistant are you to changing shape? Are you willing to take on the shape He has in mind for you, or are you set on a shape of your own? As Shaunti Feldhahn reminds us, God wants to mold us. When we are willing to let Him shape our lives, He showers us with His abundance.

God is molding and shaping you. Will you let Him be your Sacred Sculptor?

Read Romans 9:20–21.

* * * * * * * * * * * * * * * * * * * *

Sacred Sculptor, mold me. May I be pliable in Your hands.

Prayer and Praise

Worshiping needs to come before asking.
In our prayers, there needs to be more praise than petition.

Joyce Meyer

Some people only call when they want something. Their short greeting is quickly followed by a request. We know the minute we hear a certain voice on the line that we need to put up the boundaries and be ready with a reason for our yes or no. After a while, we don't like to hear from those people at all.

When we approach God, are we guilty of being like those difficult friends? "Hi God," we say, followed by, "Here's what I need from You." The privilege of even approaching God with our requests is granted to us at great cost to our Savior. The least we can do is open our prayers with worship and praise to our great God.

Adore Him. Thank Him. Praise Him. Let your mind focus on His greatness. Then bring your requests humbly to Him. He will be honored and glorified by you.

Read Psalm 150.

Lord, I praise You for Your greatness and power.
Thank You for hearing me.

Seeing His Face

*[I resolve] to search for the face of God not only
in prayer but in having no other intention
in my work, words, or sufferings.*

Mother Veronica Namoyo

Picture the homeless traveler. His clothes are dirty, and he wears no shoes. Is it possible to see God in him? Yes. Jesus looked that way at times.

Visualize a frowning boss, holding out unreasonable demands. Is it possible to see God in this situation? Yes. Jesus faced accusers who pointed and demanded. He forgave them.

Remember the sickness or the aches and pains you have struggled to overcome. Is it possible to see God in these? Yes. Jesus suffers with us.

Mother Veronica was born into a Communist family and raised by parents who denigrated faith and denied God. Yet she believed at a young age and, through her example, even these family members became followers of Jesus. She went on to set up monasteries in North Africa.

Mother Veronica resolved to find Jesus everywhere. To those who are paying prayerful attention, God shows Himself. Where will you see Him today?

Read Luke 10:25–28.

. . . .

*Holy Spirit, guide me. Help me see Jesus
in the people I meet today.*

Sweet Surrender

When difficult circumstances come into my life,
I hear God's voice saying, "Let Me be the blessed controller.
Surrender. Accept My timing. Accept My ways.
Accept My outcome. Let your trust be in Me alone."

Linda Dillow

One word in Linda's quote can be easily overlooked—the word *when*. Not *if*, but *when* difficult circumstances come into our lives, we are called to listen for God's voice. Maybe you're going through a peaceful season right now, and your load is light. What better time to start practicing? Wake up each morning and say, "Lord, I'm giving You full control of this day and all that concerns me."

And if today is full of difficult circumstances, God calls you to let Him take control. Surrender it all to Him. Accept the timing of His answers, the ways He will answer, and the outcome He has planned.

Let go, dear sister. During the good times and the bad, God lovingly calls you to trust Him alone. Begin the obedient act of falling back into His waiting arms. Trust Him. He'll catch you every time.

Read Isaiah 55:8–9.

. . . .

Precious Lord, I surrender today to Your timing,
Your ways, Your outcome.

Mirror, Mirror

*I was able to look at my weaknesses calmly, honestly
and with hope because I knew I was standing
in the presence of a Father who loved me.
Looking at Him made it easier to look at me.*

Ann Spangler

We've all had bad hair days. No matter what we do, we just can't get the hair to lay right, curl right, act right. We've all had bad hair days spiritually as well. We look in the mirror and see only weaknesses and failures glaring back at us. It's hard enough to go out in public on a bad hair day—but when we think that even our weaknesses are exposed, hopelessness begins to set in.

Ann Spangler suggests that we stop staring at our flaws and instead look calmly, honestly, and with hope at the God who made us in His image. He is good and gracious, forgiving and faithful, humble and holy, loving and loyal.

Looking at Him will make it easier to look at yourself. When you're standing in the presence of the Father who loves you, you see the beauty He sees—the beauty you are.

Read Psalm 45:11.

. . . .

Gracious Father, thank You for seeing me as beautiful.

He Will Not Let You Go

In His great wisdom, He let me realize that nowhere else
in the whole wide world, nowhere in all creation,
can I go from His presence. He wouldn't let me go.

Jan Dravecky

The six-year-old boy, angry that Mom won't give him ice cream for lunch, packs up his belongings in a plastic bag and declares that he is running away. Mom keeps an eye out, watches him head to the neighbor's home, and makes a quick phone call. Then she watches and waits. Her son will soon return. In short order, he discovers that he needs his mom, that no other place offers the comforts of home, and that Mom loves him and wants the very best for him—which doesn't include ice cream for lunch!

At times we are frustrated with God, angry at His refusal to give us what we want. We figuratively pack our bags to run away—only to discover that we cannot get away from His presence. He is watching, waiting, loving.

He loves you too much to let you go. So unpack your bags. You're home.

Read Psalm 139:7–10.

. . . .

Father, thank You for Your loving pursuit of me
in my willful wandering.

Sweet Lessons

*If I had been told what I was to learn through these
lengthy sufferings, I am afraid I would have shrunk
back in terror, and so have lost all the sweet lessons
God proposed to teach me.*

Elizabeth Prentiss

What if we could know what the future holds? It seems like a good idea. If we could know what's going to happen to us, we'd be better prepared, right?

But what if the future holds suffering? What if we discover that the coming years will bring pain, difficulty, or sorrow? To know this would perhaps cause us, as Elizabeth Prentiss says, to shrink back in terror—not wanting to take another step toward the pain.

It is much better for us not to know too much, but instead to live life fully every day. Then, when suffering comes, we trust in God's promise to supply His grace so we can endure. Beyond that, we watch for the sweet lessons He proposes to teach us in the midst of our suffering—lessons we could not learn any other way.

In your suffering, dear sister, God has sweet lessons for you. Let Him teach you.

Read Psalm 119:124.

. . . .

*Teach me the sweet lessons You have for me, Lord.
I am Your student.*

Wholly Satisfied

To be holy is to be wholly satisfied with Christ.
Above all, it is to reflect the beauty and the splendor
of our holy Lord in this dark world. In pursuing holiness, you
will fulfill and experience all that God
had in mind when He created you.

Nancy DeMoss Wolgemuth

The flame of a lit candle is inconsequential during the day. But take a candle into a deep cave, and its light will make the difference between safety or stumbling, between finding your way or being lost, even between life or death.

Shine the candle into your life. What do you see? In a dark world, secret and habitual sins can be hidden. But if you seek holiness, your candle will show where Christ needs to cleanse your life of sin, clear away the baggage of the past, and help you become more like Him. Like a candle in a cave, the holiness Christ gives will keep you safe, help you find your way, and reflect the beauty and splendor of Jesus into a dark world.

To walk in holiness is to experience all that God had in mind when He created you. You will find that you want nothing more.

Read Leviticus 11:44.

. . . .

Father, may I desire holiness more than anything else.

Kind Words

To be candid without ostentation or design—
to take the good of everybody's character and make it still better,
and say nothing of the bad—belongs to you alone.

Jane Austen

What fills our conversation about others? Are we full of praise about others' goodness? Or are we eager to gossip about their faults?

The words of Jane Austen remind us that, while we have our opinions, we would do well to speak of the good in people's character and say nothing of the bad. When talking to friends, coworkers, neighbors, or church members, the choice belongs to us alone to see the strengths in others and remain silent about their weaknesses. Usually a person's weakness is glaring anyway, and our help is not needed in bringing attention to it. Would we want other people talking about our glaring weaknesses—the weaknesses of which we are painfully aware?

Christ knows our every shortcoming, and thankfully, He wants us, welcomes us, and loves us. Let your words about others be uplifting and kind, reflecting Jesus's love for you.

Read Proverbs 16:28.

. . . .

Today, Lord, let my words about others be positive,
helpful, and encouraging.

God's Love Letters

I am a little pencil in the hand of a writing God
who is sending a love letter to the world.
Mother Teresa

There's something about a handwritten note that means so much more than even the kindest email or text message. A thank you, an "I love you," or a note that says "I'm thinking of you," when written by hand above your signature, sends a special message to the receiver: "You are worth it."

You are like the precious pencil in God's hand. God is sending a love letter to the world—and you are that personalized note. He sends you when someone needs love, tenderness, companionship, encouragement, courage, or kindness. Your small stroke of a smile or your willingness to erase others' mistakes sends an unmistakable message of God's love. A pencil? Seems small and unimportant and certainly not high-tech, but it is oh so powerful.

Like Mother Teresa, you are a little pencil in God's hand, writing a love letter to the world. What message is He sending through you today?

Read 1 John 3:11.

God, use me to write Your love on the hearts of others today.

A Cup in the Morning

*Imagine how different our days would be if we had
our cups filled by Christ first thing in the morning.*

Beth Moore

*T*he alarm rings. As our minds wake from the fuzziness of
slumber, thoughts of the day come rushing in. The day
ahead may hold some unpleasant tasks; perhaps our to-do list
is so long it makes us tired before we even begin. In any case,
some mornings, we'd rather stay in bed so we don't have to face
the day at all.

But as Beth Moore states, imagine how different our days
would be if we had our cups filled by Christ first thing in the
morning!

When Christ fills our cups, He gives us His love, joy, peace
and patience. We're able to be kind, good, faithful, gentle. And
hey, a little self-control might come in handy at an opportune
moment as well!

Christ wants to fill your cup to the brim. He knows just
what you need for the day ahead.

Read Psalm 5:3.

Fill my cup, Lord. You know just what I need for today.

Unwrap Your Gifts

Often we do not know our own gifts.
That's why it's a great help to self-knowledge
if we have family and friends who can tell us honestly,
"This is what you do well."

Ingrid Trobisch

Can you remember a moment during your childhood when a trusted adult noticed that you had an aptitude for something? Perhaps your sixth grade teacher encouraged your interest in science, or a piano teacher cheered on your musical talent. Perhaps a grandparent affirmed your communication skills. Until that person noticed, you may not have been fully aware that something special was happening in your life.

We all want to serve God well, and we want to use the gifts He has given us. But what, exactly, are those gifts? And how will we know?

We will know when we hear it from those who know us best. When they truly compliment something we do well, something we already love to do, we'll know we have discovered a gift from God.

Then the next question is, "Where, God, do You want me to use my gifts for You?"

Read 1 Corinthians 12:4–7.

Show me my gifts, Lord, and show me where to use them.

Small Things

Do some small things with great love. Help somebody. Maybe just smile . . . and you will find Him.

Mother Teresa

Although Mother Teresa did "big things" by founding worldwide centers for the poor and devoting her life to serving the sick, she encouraged others to do small, everyday actions with great love. It is the *love* that counts, not the scope of our work.

God may call some of us to great acts of service in the public eye, as He did Mother Teresa. Most of us, however, won't gain national attention for what we do. That doesn't make our service any less valuable. The meal you deliver to a sick neighbor provides for her family. Your friendly smile to the cashier brightens a tough day at work. The grouchy family member who comes home to the smell of cookies baking remembers that you love him.

The small things add up. They matter to the people who receive them.

When you pour out love, you find Jesus. And others find Him too.

Read 2 John 5–6.

Father, help me to be willing to do the small things for others with love.

Whom Do You Serve?

Here's the secret to serving with the right attitude:
take your eyes off the physical people you
are serving and place your eyes solely on the One
whom you must ultimately serve.

Priscilla Shirer

It's workday at your church, and you're assigned the lowliest, most unpleasant job on the list. You get to deep-clean the bathrooms.

Not very glamorous.

The chemical smell is only a little worse than, well, the typical bathroom smells. Dirt is ground in. You can't imagine how any place could get so dirty. In the middle of wiping around the third toilet, you realize that this is just going to get dirty again (quickly), and no one is going to notice or recognize your hard work.

And then, by the fourth toilet, Jesus has let you know that it's not about you, it's not about toilets, and it's not about the rest of the church members. It's about serving. And it's about Him.

God is pleased when we consider our service for others as service for Him. Even when it includes cleaning bathrooms.

In the end, serving Him is what matters most.

Read Ephesians 6:7.

O God, teach me to enjoy serving others as a way of serving You.

Find Your Way

I thought I had lost my way. Actually,
I did lose my way—in order to follow God's way.

Jan Dravecky

*P*icture yourself in a rowboat in the middle of a large lake. The sun is setting. You see your destination on the shore, so you grab your oars and paddle toward it. Suddenly fog feathers around you, getting denser as dusk settles. You can no longer see the shore. You paddle in what you think is the right direction. You should have reached the shore by now! Panic rises in your throat.

Then you hear a voice calling from a distance behind you. The shore is the other way! You turn and paddle toward the voice, the only way home.

Sometimes we have to lose our way so we can find God's way. Sometimes we need Him to call us from the fog and turn us around.

God has a plan for you, a place for you, and a journey for you.

Listen. Can you hear Him calling?

Read Luke 19:10.

* * * * * * * * * * * * * * * * * * *

Show me the way, Lord. I'm looking forward
to going where You lead!

Valley of Shadow

As you come to dark places in your life,
just reach out for the hand of the Shepherd.
Helen Steiner Rice

She held him tightly, mourning his numbered days as cancer devoured the body of her loving husband. During those dark days, very little light or laughter crept into her world.

Life has its dark, scary places. Nobody welcomes emotional or physical pain, disappointment, or death. At one time or another, we all walk through a valley of shadow.

The bright spot is assurance that we can reach out to a gentle Shepherd to guide us through. We can rest in His goodness even in the badness of a situation. During the days—or weeks or months—when you cannot see the light or do not know what to do or say, simply reach out for His hand. He's there. He promised to never leave you, even when you walk through the valley of shadow. He's there to comfort, sustain, empower, and provide for you.

He may not lighten your dark places, but He will lighten your load.

Read Psalm 23.

. . . .

I'm reaching out for You, gentle Shepherd.
Take my hand through this dark valley.

That First Step

God has designed a life plan for each one of us.
It was custom fitted to our talents and personality,
and it usually involves a step of faith.
But that step, the first one, is always up to us.

Martha Bolton

*G*od has a job for you to do that no one else can do. No one else is so perfectly suited by way of talents, personality, background, or life experiences. You are unique, created by God for a purpose. As you walk with Him through life, He will show you exactly what He created you to do.

But that first step? That step of faith that tries something you've never tried before, that takes you out of your comfort zone, that asks something beyond what you think you can do—*that* step is all up to you.

Will you take that first step? Like a toddler who gingerly lets go of the edge of the couch, settles shaky legs, and then ventures out across the room one wobbly step at a time, so you need to let go and take the first step into God's plan.

It's up to you.

Read Jeremiah 10:23.

. . . .

One step at a time, Lord. Guide me one step at a time.

Loving Service

Do not build towers without a foundation, for our Lord
does not care so much for the importance
of our works as for the love with which they are done.

Teresa of Avila

We want to do great and important things for God. Nothing wrong with that; it's certainly a noble desire. Yet even if we are given the opportunity to do great things—to give large amounts of money, build churches, speak to thousands, introduce many to salvation—the Lord is looking more closely at our attitude than at the works themselves. He is looking at the foundation on which our tower of works is built; He is looking for an attitude of love.

Those great things we do for God—are they done for attention, accolades, a name on a building, an award? Or are they done simply out of gratitude to God and love for our fellow human beings?

Your works—whether large or small—when done in love, are of great value to your Lord.

Read Mark 9:41.

. . . .

Lord, help me to serve others from
the solid foundation of Your love.

Content with Now

I have always, essentially, been waiting.
Waiting to become something else, waiting to be
that person I always thought I was on the verge of becoming,
waiting for that life I thought I would have.

Shauna Niequist

Some people spend their entire lives waiting. Days pass, people come and go, relationships wither, opportunities disappear—all because they've kept their focus on the horizon, waiting for something better. If we wait for the life that we thought we would have, we miss the life right in front of us. That would be a sad legacy indeed.

It is hard to just be happy in the now, especially if *now* doesn't look like you had hoped or planned. When planted, the seeds of discontent will grow into full-fledged bitterness and despair. How much better to look around at the now, be content with all that God has given, and thank Him for the blessings He has provided.

Let God take what you thought life would be and give you a new focus. Contentment will get you there.

Read 1 Timothy 6:6.

Father, I want to be content with all that You have given.
Thank You.

Fear Not

By our worrying and fretting, we are really saying,
"I don't believe in any God who can help me,
and I do not trust Him." . . . We need to develop
a sense of dependence on the fatherliness of God.
Catherine Marshall

The role of father is to be protector and provider. Our heavenly Father does this for us. We have nothing to fear when we truly believe in Him. We know we can trust Him to both protect and provide.

Why, then, all this anxiety? Why do we spend so much time afraid—wondering if we will be provided for, cared for, protected? Do we not understand that when we worry and fret, we are basically telling God that we don't trust Him to handle our problems?

If we trust we don't need to worry . . . do we?

When anxiety creeps in, as it does for all of us, we can use it as a wake-up call. Worry time is the perfect time to surrender. We need our Father. He has not left us. Our Father knows our needs.

Are you worrying and fretting today? Depend on your heavenly Father. He will protect. He will provide.

Read Luke 12:22–26.

Heavenly Father, I place my trust in You. I depend on You.

Open the Door

*I know that disobedience can lock and bolt the door
against God's still, small voice.*

Joyce Huggett

We can feel justified in doing our own thing—and few people can tell us we're wrong if we've already made up our minds. We don't want advice, so we avoid anyone who offers it. We close our Bibles. We excuse ourselves from worship and sermons at church, counting on God's grace to make up for our losses; hoping against hope that, even in our disobedience, He'll cut us some slack because He knows what we're up against.

All the while we ignore the possibility that our disobedience is causing our hearts to grow hard against God and His still, small voice. We choose to go our own way. We shut ourselves inside our disobedience, locking and bolting the door.

Oh, we can stay in there as long as we like. Eventually, however, we'll find ourselves miserable, missing God. Then we hear a quiet, gentle knock.

It's Him!

Read Revelation 3:20.

. . . .

*Lord, may I always be able to hear Your gentle voice
and Your quiet knock.*

Stand Up

Right is right, even if no one else does it.
Juliette Low

*E*verybody's doing it!" Children are famous for presenting that argument when they want permission to have their way. But moms are just as famous for their retort. In fact, you can almost hear mothers across the continent speaking in unison, "If everyone jumped off a cliff, would you jump too?"

Going against the flow is uncomfortable. It's hard to buck the system and even harder to stand up for what is right when no one else stands with you. These days it seems that fewer and fewer people stand for what is right. In your situation, you may indeed be the only one!

Be assured that you are not alone. When you take a stand for what is right, Jesus is beside you, providing strength and fortitude to stay strong. And you never know the influence you have on others. Your decision to do what is right may inspire others to do the same!

Read Matthew 7:13–14.

. . . .

Lord, guide me to do what is right,
even if I have to do it alone.

Lean on Me

*The special people God gives us along the way make us
stronger to face the trials of an ugly world.*

Gracia Burnham

We are never alone. Even when it might feel that way, God
puts people in our lives at strategic moments to comfort
us, to give us encouragement, and to help us find strength
to face the next trial. The Bible has many examples: Adam
had Eve, Moses had Aaron, David had Jonathan, Mary had
Elizabeth, Paul had Timothy.

When times are tough, God will be there. He'll send
messengers at the moments when we need them most. They
may be strangers, trusted friends, or unexpected acquaintances. They may not be what we expect.

Be open, dear sister, to the words and touch of those
around you. In this sometimes ugly world, they may just be
exactly who—and what—you need.

And be open to how God may use you. *You* may be that
special person in someone else's life, providing them strength
to make it through their day.

Read Galatians 6:2.

*Make me receptive, Father, to the people
You send into my life.*

Daily Blessings

*God is offering Himself to you daily, and the rate
of exchange is fixed: your sins for His forgiveness,
your hurt for His balm of healing, your sorrow for His joy.*

Barbara Johnson

God offers Himself to you daily. Think of it! Who else does that? Who else comes running whenever you have a need? Your mother? Your father? A dear sister? A friend? And even if you have many loved ones who are faithful to assist you, how much can they really do? Their efforts are limited by their humanity.

But, think of it. God, the Creator of the universe, the Ruler of heaven and earth, watches over you every moment of every day. And nothing is impossible for Him. He stands ready to exchange your sins for His forgiveness, your pain for His healing, and your sorrow for His abundant joy. God will walk you through your problems and meet your needs according to His wisdom and His timing. He chose you, bought you, calls you by name, and enjoys taking care of you.

Take Him up on it.

Read Psalm 86:1–4.

*I praise You, Lord God my Father, for watching over me.
I worship You.*

Priceless

*Forgive me for accusing You of making a mistake when
You made me. From now on, I accept with joy Your decision
to make me average. I surrender myself to You.*

Kay Warren

We've all played the comparison game. *She* has longer eyelashes than I do; *she's* more organized; *she's* in better shape; *she's* a gifted speaker. Why do we insist on playing a game that we always lose?

When we play comparisons, we're also accusing God of messing up when He made us. That, by extension, says He's not perfect—and at that point we're on very thin ice indeed.

Let's decide to accept ourselves *exactly* how God made us. We may feel that our flaws make us merely average, but as any collector knows, the imperfections are often what make a work most valuable.

God loves you—flaws and all. When you surrender to Him and stop comparing yourself to others, He is free to use the gifts and abilities He implanted in you for His glory.

Thank Him today for how He made you, flaws included. You are priceless.

Read Isaiah 64:8.

. . . .

*Help me surrender my self-critical spirit
and appreciate how You created me.*

Let Him Work in You

God is more interested in teaching me through
a situation than in using me in a situation.
Carole Mayhall

We desperately want to be out working, serving, and doing for God, but at times we feel sidetracked. Wrapped up in raising children, housebound with an illness, separated from projects and people we care about—we feel that we are not doing anything at all for God's kingdom. If He's not working through us, then, well, nothing good can be happening. We want to be anywhere but where God has us.

Instead, God says, "Wait, child. Sit quietly. Let Me work *in* you." As our hearts catch up to that understanding, the dissatisfaction and disappointment dissipate. Restlessness and grumbling are replaced with praise and thanksgiving to God. Our minds and spirits open to hear God's instruction. Our hearts soften to soak up God's love.

With God working in you, you're never sidelined, never useless. He will teach you wherever He has you.

Read Psalm 37:7.

I put my desires before You, God,
ready to receive Your instruction.

Enjoy His Goodness

[God] is absolute good. . . . The more we contemplate Him,
the more we enjoy of His good.
Julia Ward Howe

Absolute good. What does it look like? Such perfection is unfathomable in our imperfect world, where even simple goodness seems to be in short supply.

Yet absolute good does indeed exist in the person of God Almighty. And He invites us to enjoy that goodness by enjoying Him, by drawing close to Him. As we contemplate His goodness, we let it sink into our lives. God's goodness is so overwhelming, so rich, so immense, that our very contemplation immerses us in that goodness.

God has given us many ways to know Him and see facets of who He is: creation, His Word, stories from fellow Christians of His faithfulness, goodness, and care. Now add contemplation of His goodness to the list.

In these moments, contemplate God's goodness to you. You will be filled to overflowing. Take that goodness and spread it around your world today.

Read 1 Peter 2:9.

You are absolute goodness, dear Lord.
I immerse myself in You.

In His Sight

How wonderful that we serve a God who formed us and,
therefore, understands our frailty and susceptibility,
yet has grace-filled plans for us.

Patsy Clairmont

How often do we go around disqualifying ourselves from God's plans for our lives? We say to ourselves, "Now I really messed up. There's no way God can use me now," or, "I've sinned so badly, God is not going to want anything more to do with me." We can accept that He'll forgive us, but we cannot imagine that He can still use us for His purposes and glory.

That's a lie, dear sister. Not only does He forgive—He knows our weaknesses and *still* has glorious, God-sized plans for our lives.

For *your* life.

Don't let your past, not even your yesterday, dictate your future. Instead, let His past—His perfect atonement for your sins on the cross—decide who you are and what you will do. He died to deal with sin. *Every* sin.

He can and will use you for His purposes. You just need to let Him.

Read Acts 9:13–15.
. . . .
You know me and my faults.
Thank You that You can still use me.

Chasing Out the Pests

*The true test of walking in the Spirit
will not be the way we act, but the way
we react to the daily frustrations of life.*

Beverly LaHaye

When we can anticipate problems, plan for events, and manage our time, it's easy to be on our best behavior. But oh, those other times. Those pesky irritations and annoyances that pop up when we're least prepared for them. A traffic jam, a ringing telephone, a too-long line at the checkout, a misplaced purse, or something that just doesn't go our way. If we'd been able to prepare, we might have known how to act. Instead, we react to these situations with complaints, muttering, impatience, and anger.

Actions *and* reactions tell the story of our walk with God. What is God revealing to you today about your walk with Him? Is there something He wants you to repent of, change, learn, or make right? What a comfort it is that the Holy Spirit helps as we pick ourselves up, dust ourselves off, and try again to deal with the daily frustrations of life!

Read Galatians 5:16.

God, help me to walk conscious of You today as I react to life.

Ask God First

The principle "make no decision without prayer"
keeps me from rushing in and committing myself before
I consult God. It guards me against people-pleasing.

Elizabeth George

How many times have you been asked to do something—a perfectly God-honoring, mission-fulfilling task—and you agreed only because you knew that's what the person asking wanted to hear? And how many times have you regretted that decision as soon as you hung up the phone? Consider this: that task may have been a burden you were not meant to bear.

Suppose you do as Elizabeth George suggests: make no decision without prayer. Imagine not feeling the pressure to say *yes* when everything in you is shouting *no*. Imagine the joy of conferring with God in the decision-making process. Imagine the relief when He says, "No, this is not something I want you to do," or the excitement when He says, "Yes, I will enable you to do this task. It's perfect for you."

No more people-pleasing. Your job is to be God-pleasing. That's what matters most.

Read Philippians 4:6–7.

. . . .

Lord, remind me to make no decision
without talking to You first.

The View from the Pit

There is no pit so deep that His love is not deeper still.

Corrie ten Boom

*I*n the pit, we are enveloped by darkness. It's cold. Dank. And very lonely. Our cries go unheard, and eventually all we can do is whimper into the darkness, hoping against hope that someone will hear, someone will call down to us from above, someone will find a way to rescue us. But as our tears fall to the ground, we know that we may be here for a long time.

Where is God?

The truth, dear sister, is that He is here. In the pit. He knows the trial that has sent you into this pit of darkness. Abandonment, uselessness, grief, fear, depression. He desires to help you out of the pit. To raise you back to the sunshine and fresh air. To refresh you to serve again.

Corrie ten Boom lived it. "There is no pit so deep that His love is not deeper still." Grab onto God and don't let go.

Read Psalm 40:2.

. . . .

This pit is dark, Lord, but I am holding on to You.

Lead Us

Savior, like a shepherd lead us, much we need
Thy tender care. In Thy pleasant pastures feed us,
for our use Thy folds prepare. . . . Blessed Jesus,
blessed Jesus! Thou hast bought us, Thine we are.

Dorothy Thrupp

Savior, like a shepherd lead us. Call us each morning to You. Gather us together. As You set off into the day, we simply follow.

We watch You as You move ahead of us. We trust You. You will take us to pastures of green grass so we can eat. You will be careful to bring us to still waters, for You know that we can easily be swept away by swiftly flowing streams. You will not take us on paths too rocky for our hooves to handle or too steep for us to climb. You will tenderly care for us should we get caught in the briars or stumble on the path. And, when the sun sets, You will return us safely to the fold.

You bought us. You know us. We are Yours.

Your Shepherd calls you today to follow. You can trust Him wherever He leads.

Read Isaiah 40:11

. . . .

I trust You, Good Shepherd, to lead me today.

Daily Surrender

True surrender is not a single action but a posture in life,
yielding ourselves—our whole selves—to God.

Margaret Feinberg

Surrender. The word brings to mind wounded, bloodied, battle-weary soldiers trudging back to camp, shoulders hunched and faces downcast. Surrender can mean humiliation and failure.

But surrender can also be a positive word. Surrendering our lives to God is not the result of losing a battle. God does not intend humiliation and failure for us, but rather life in His abundance. When we surrender—we win! This new picture of surrender is not of heads hanging in failure but of hands raised in victory.

And as Margaret Feinberg suggests, this surrender is not a single action. We must surrender daily. Each morning before our feet hit the floor, we surrender to God, asking Him to take over, to walk us through the battles, to bring His victory into our lives.

Wave the white flag. Surrender daily.

In the end, you win.

Read Psalm 25:4–5.

Lord, I trade my posture of defeat for one of victory
by surrendering to You.

The Work on Our Doorstep

Let us never say, "God has given me nothing to do."
He has. It lies on our doorstep.
Do it, and He will show you something else.
Elisabeth Elliot

"There's nothing to do," the child whines, only to have mom answer, "Well, I can *find* you something to do." Moms have a great way of finding chores for a bored child; there is always something that needs to be done.

It's the same with our Christian lives. We look around, bored, thinking that God has given us nothing to do. However, as Elisabeth Elliot says, the next job we can do for Him is right on our doorstep. The job may not seem very spiritual. It may not even be noticeable. But if God has placed it in front of you, chances are He wants you to get it done for Him.

It just boils down to paying attention, listening, and keeping an eye out at the front door. You never know what God's going to bring your way.

In God's kingdom, there is always something to do.

Read Ecclesiastes 9:10.

God, help me to see and do the work before me.

Home

Old homes, new homes, tiny cottages, magnificent palaces,
little huts, big tents, a sleeping bag on a wanderer's back,
or a trailer—whatever the home of the believer,
the astonishing and breathtaking promise
is that God will live with us.

Edith Schaeffer

When He came to dwell among us, God chose to be born in a stable—a place most of us wouldn't even consider sleeping! Yet another sign, dear sister, of the astonishing lengths God has gone to . . . to be with us!

By choosing a stable, God also sent another message: He cares about our hearts; not how clean our houses are. We don't need to meet a certain standard of living. He doesn't care if our house is not as nice as the one next door. He'll even join us in the tent! You see, He simply wants to *be* with us. He wants to experience life as it is *with us*, to live with us and spend time with us wherever we live. That fact takes our breath away!

Beloved, is Jesus knocking at your door? You can let Him in—no need to vacuum first.

Read John 14:16–17.

Father, I am astonished that You want
to spend time with me. Thank You.

Invincible

I felt invincible. My strength was that of a giant.
God was certainly standing by me.

Carrie Nation

*A*s women, we sometimes feel it isn't ladylike to be assertive or bold. We may think it's not our place to speak out. Scripture, however, reveals many examples where a woman's boldness was right, necessary, and appropriate. Deborah led an army; Ruth followed Naomi to a new land; Esther put her life on the line; Mary offered her finest perfume to wash Jesus's feet. God blessed those who obeyed His prompting and acted on their convictions.

Just as Carrie Nation felt invincible, you, too, can do mighty—perhaps historic—acts through Him. When God calls you, He will give you the strength of a giant. He will stand beside you. He will empower you to do His will. Your faith in God will result in the boldness and confidence you need to do what may seem to be impossible.

With God beside you, you are invincible.

Read 2 Samuel 22:30.

. . . .

Lord, grant me strength today to say and do what is right.

Drink Deeply

Come to Him and drink. Drink deeply; keep on drinking;
let Him quench your thirst. And then,
watch as rivers of living water flow out through you
to quench the thirst of those around you.
Nancy DeMoss Wolgemuth

The ice is clinking in the pitcher of freshly squeezed lemonade. You're invited! The door is open. The welcome mat is out. The table is set.

Come, join Him at the table. Stay awhile. Savor His Word, rest in His presence, and listen for His voice. Let God quench the thirst of your soul like water hydrates the body after an intense workout, like a deep breath in the mountain air clears your lungs, like a swim in a beautiful, cool spring rejuvenates your tired limbs.

Are you thirsty today? Thirsty for meaning in life? Thirsty for love that will not fail? Thirsty for peace or joy or contentment? Come to Him and drink. The well is deep; the supply endless. And then, once you've drunk your fill, that living water flows out through you to the thirsty souls around you.

Who will you refresh today?

Read John 7:37–38.

Quench my thirst today, God.
Then let me refresh someone else.

Time to Be Still

I sit on my favorite rock, looking over the brook,
to take time away from busyness, time to be. . . .
It's something we all need for our spiritual health,
and often we don't take enough of it.

Madeleine L'Engle

So many people try to cram forty hours of activity into each twenty-four-hour day. That seems to be the expectation of the world. Yet our souls cry out, "Stop! Be quiet. Seek silence. Just *be*." When we take a break from the constant running, a door opens into heaven.

Attend to the mysteries of your soul by quieting your mind before the Lord. Nothing is more valuable than this time with God. No schedules, no chores, no plans are more important than the need to sit in the presence of His glory.

Create a space for quiet. Create a place for prayer. Maybe it's that favorite rock by the brook or a favorite chair in your bedroom. Wherever it is, that is your place for taking time to *be* and to renew your spiritual health.

The paradoxical truth is that you're too busy *not* to take time for God.

Read Mark 1:35.

. . . .

I just want to sit here and be with You, Lord.
Thank You for this quiet time.

Someone Who Listens

Descartes said, "Because I think, I am." Because I am,
I pray. . . . We do this not . . . to curry favor for some
hoped for life beyond this one. We do this because
we've got to talk to somebody.

Marjorie Holmes

The urge to talk to the Creator is part of who we are. It was created in us by the One who made us. Because we are—because we are alive and breathing—we pray. As Marjorie Holmes explains, we pray not to get favor but because we simply must talk to someone.

Sometimes the pain goes so deep, we just don't want to share it with others. At times, in the still quiet of a sleepless night, we need to take our worries and fears—the ones that don't seem quite so troubling in the daylight—to someone who cares and understands. Then there are the days when our hearts are so full of joy, they are about to burst, and we've got to share it with the One we know is responsible.

Do you need to talk to someone? Pray. God is listening.

Read Lamentations 3:55–58.

Lord, I bring You my troubles. I trust in Your help.

Knowing His Love

The greatest honor we can give Almighty God
is to live gladly because of the knowledge of His love.

Julian of Norwich

There's nothing quite like being in love. When we're in love and know that love is returned, the whole world is rosy. Love is a gift that causes even the most mundane aspects of life to seem wondrous. We even smile at others more.

The gospel is a love story—the story of God's love for a wayward people, poignantly displayed through the death of His Son on the cross for our sins. The knowledge of this precious love lifts the soul and imbues even mundane aspects of our lives with a patina of richness.

A love like that deserves a response. We can best acknowledge this love by honoring the Lover. We can offer Him praise. We can serve others in the overflow of that love.

You are loved. Bask in the thought. Then honor the One who loves you by living in the knowledge of His amazing love.

Read 1 John 4:7–12.

Lord, in gratitude for Your love,
I wish to honor You with my life.

Reaching for the Stars

A Christian has no business being satisfied with mediocrity.
He's supposed to reach for the stars. Why not?
He's not on his own any more. He has God's help now.

Catherine Marshall

Look up," Scripture tells us. Look to the stars and remember who made them. Look to the mountains and worship their Creator.

Much of the activity of our lives requires daily, repetitive tasks that keep us focused on earth. We can easily get sucked in to mediocrity. But God has a higher calling for us. He wants us to do everything with our best effort—even beyond that, to reach for the stars. That means as we work and serve our Lord, we refuse to be satisfied with the mediocre. We refuse to just get by, to do just enough. We are so passionate about serving our Lord that we want to always do our best work.

Don't worry, sister. This is not a new standard for you to attempt to reach. You have God's help now. That's what enables you to reach the stars in the first place!

Read Psalm 121:1–2.

Father, in all I do, let me reach for the stars!

The Little Things

Always be faithful in little things,
for in them our strength lies.

Mother Teresa

*L*ittle things matter. Too often, we focus on the big things of our faith and miss the little things. But as Mother Teresa explains, we need to first be faithful in the little things. That gives us the strength for the "big" things.

It's subtle, but we can find ourselves rationalizing some sins—"I deserve a break . . . No one will know . . . I'm not hurting anyone." But those very choices eat away at our character, undermining the strength we need to handle the powerful temptations, the weighty responsibilities. If we can't handle the small things, it follows that we cannot handle the big things either.

So focus on the small stuff. Quiet honesty. Hidden acts of kindness. Willingly turning away from temptation even when no one else will know.

Only faithfulness there lays the foundation for faithfulness in the big areas of life.

The little things really do add up.

Read Song of Songs 2:15.

. . . .

Lord, help me to be faithful in the little things.

Priceless

*Progress has a price; and becoming a person
who never gives up will cost you.*
Joyce Meyer

What might it cost us to walk closer with Jesus, to move forward and deeper in our relationship with Him? Might we have to lose a friend who is holding us back? Might we have to set aside some habits that we know are detrimental to our spiritual growth? Lose a few extra minutes of sleep in order to have a daily quiet time? Risk annoying a family member who thinks we've jumped overboard?

Moving forward always has a price. Risks are involved. Often we enter uncharted territory. Dangers may come our way. Like Pilgrim in the classic book, *Pilgrim's Progress,* our journeys to the Celestial City take us through all manner of sloughs and valleys.

But the only way to get where we're going is to never give up. To walk closer with Jesus is priceless. The cost isn't worth counting.

Read Matthew 16:24–28.

Jesus, I want to never give up as I draw closer to You.

Give It Your All

*Lord, teach me to worship You with my whole heart
the way You want me to. Make me a true worshiper.
May praise and worship of You
be my first response to every circumstance.*

Stormie Omartian

It would do us good to consider our first responses to every situation we encounter in a given day. First response to no milk left in the fridge for breakfast. First response to a traffic jam. First response to plans changed due to a child's sudden cough. First response to a perceived slight. First response to the long line at the store to buy the needed milk.

What if our first response to *every circumstance* was praise and worship? Is that even possible?

It is when you ask God to help you. He can show you what worship with all your heart in every circumstance looks like and feels like.

When you worship God with your whole heart in grateful contemplation of His majesty and love, there's little room for self-pity or anger—those typical first responses. Instead, God gets in and infuses even the frustrating situations with renewed grace.

Read Psalm 71:14.

Teach me to praise You today in every circumstance.

Age of Bitterness

Forgiveness may be excruciating for a moment.
Anger and bitterness are excruciating for a lifetime.

Beth Moore

*E*veryone avoids her angry eyes. She enters a room and looks at no one. She sits alone in the back. She glares straight ahead. One would think the hurtful incident happened weeks or a few months ago.

"My, she's aged since I last saw her."

"I'd like to talk with her, but the look on her face is never welcoming."

"It's been twenty-four years . . . ."

The pain she felt had become rock-hard anger and bitterness, sucking away her life. The person who hurt her had moved on—for right or wrong—but she was stuck in her emotional pit, hurting only herself.

How much better if she had been willing to forgive twenty-four years ago. So much life she's missed in the meantime.

Forgiveness helps *you* move on.

Read Hebrews 12:14–15.

. . . .

Jesus, show me when I need to forgive.

Great Discipline

Greatness is never achieved nor dreams realized
apart from great discipline.

Kay Arthur

Behind the few seconds of a gymnast's vault stand hours, weeks, and years of training. For many hours a day, she practiced running and vaulting. She landed hard a few times, developed some bruises, and went back to try again. Run, vault. Run, vault. Run, vault. She practiced all those years so that her five seconds of running and vaulting might bring home an Olympic medal.

She will be the first to tell you that greatness and dreams cannot be realized without discipline.

We do not all have Olympic dreams or Olympic abilities, but we all have God-given gifts. We are responsible to discipline ourselves to develop those gifts for His glory. The greatness we achieve and the dreams we realize may not put our pictures on a cereal box, but we will accomplish what God had in mind when He created us.

And that is enough.

Read Romans 12:6–8.

. . . .

Lord, guide me to have the discipline to develop
the gifts You gave me.

Close to the Shepherd

*Sometimes it is the simple act of grazing that gets
a sheep into trouble. Nibble a little here, a little there,
a little more over in another area, and pretty soon,
they are far from the shepherd. And then a lion comes.*

Francine Rivers

The grazing sheep has its eyes focused on the ground, the next blade of grass, a little more over there, just a few more steps to the next tasty patch. Before long, the sheep looks up and finds it has wandered far from the shepherd.

We are so much like sheep! We have our eyes focused only a few inches in front of our nose. We like this, we want this, we need this. We just keep moving along to whatever comes next. Finally, we look up and realize that we have strayed far from our Shepherd.

How can we avoid this? We take our steps with our eyes always on the Shepherd. We make sure that no new "patch of grass" is distancing us too far from Him.

The grass might look greener out there, beyond the Shepherd's eye. But think again—because out there is where the lions wait.

Read Psalm 79:13.

. . . .

*Shepherd, keep me ever close to You; bring me back
when I try to roam.*

Come Away

"Come, come," He saith, "O soul oppressed and weary,
Come to the shadows of My desert rest,
Come walk with Me far from life's babbling discords,
And peace shall breathe like music in thy breast."

Harriet Beecher Stowe

"Come away with me," Jesus invites. "Let's spend some time together and talk. Your soul will find peace." And He set us an example of doing just that, for He Himself got away from the hubbub and the hustle and bustle of the crowds, away even from His friends, in order to find a quiet place to talk with His Father.

Do you have a quiet place, a safe place where you can go and meet with God, undistracted by the noise of the world? Dear sister, if Jesus needed to get away, how much more do we need to escape to truly hear our Savior's voice! It may be early morning, late at night, in a room in our home, at the library, or in the park.

Your Savior will meet you wherever you are, so come away to a place where you can listen.

Read Matthew 14:23.

Jesus, in this quiet place I want to spend some time with You.

Choose Him

He could have roared on top of a mountain,
but He whispered in the voice of a baby. He could have
ordered our obedience; instead He calls for our hearts.
Sheila Walsh

From the tiniest microscopic creature to the farthest galaxies—God is the creator of all. We exist because He allowed us to.

As such, does He not have the right to demand our love and obedience? Indeed, He had every right to roar from the top of the mountain and demand that we obey Him *or else*. Instead, He decided to let us choose. Instead of yelling at us from a mountaintop, He whispered to us with the voice of his Son, born to save us. Instead of ordering us to obey, He woos us to love.

We choose to respond because we see eyes brimming with tenderness. We willingly comply because our souls are captivated by His grace. We obey because it shows that we love the One who lavishes love on us.

God wants you to *choose* Him today. That's how much He loves you.

Read Joshua 24:15.

Thank You, Lord, for loving me. You've captured my heart.

Following God's Example

*Patience withholds: It withholds vengeance, revenge,
and retaliation, and endures instead. It endures ill treatment,
it refuses to be angry, and it desires the offender's good.*

Elizabeth George

When a friend hurts you more deeply than an enemy ever could, when harsh words cut like daggers, when coworkers accuse—what should you do? Elizabeth George suggests withholding vengeance, revenge, and retaliation. She says we should patiently endure ill treatment, refuse to be angry, and desire the offender's good when situations arise that are beyond our control.

But how can we do that when the wound still bleeds and the anger still burns? The healing begins when we realize what God has done for us. He sent His only Son to pay the penalty for our sins. When we trusted in Jesus, God wiped our slate clean. He hurled our iniquities into the depths of the sea. He remembers our sins no more.

The more fully we understand what God has done on our behalf, the better we'll be able to treat others with patience.

After all, how many times has God been patient with you?

Read Romans 2:1–4.

Lord, help me to forgive others just as You have forgiven me.

Stay Close

God comes looking for us and brings us home,
away from the danger we got ourselves into.
He loves us so much that He doesn't want
to lose even one of us.

Tracie Peterson

When a shepherd discovers a sheep is missing, he can stand and shake his head over that stupid animal. He might call out the sheep's name but then give up on it if it doesn't come. But a shepherd who cares about his sheep goes out in search of the creature who has gone astray. He knows the sheep may be lost, stuck, or in danger from a predator. He will keep looking until he finds it.

Jesus, our Great Shepherd, doesn't give up when He calls and we don't answer. He doesn't leave us to make our own way home. He doesn't stand and scold when He finds us stuck in thorns after we've wandered away. He tenderly pulls us out of the thorn bush and offers medicine for our wounds.

Oh, that we would learn that the best place is to stay close by the Shepherd's side.

Read John 10:11–15.

. . . .

My Shepherd, thank You for caring for me enough
to look for me when I wander.

Immeasurable Love

Incredible, isn't it? To imagine God's love reaching across
the boundaries of time, encircling us in His ceaseless embrace.
Do you yearn to feel His heavenly arms around you?
Holding you, comforting you, cherishing you?

Liz Curtis Higgs

*I*t is truly beyond our comprehension. A God who loves us. A God not of stone or marble but a living being. A God who existed before time itself.

This God reaches across time and space to encircle us in a ceaseless embrace. This love is beyond our imagination, so He shows it in thousands of ways He knows we can process. Sense His beaming face when you help a neighbor. Feel His comfort in a friend's kind words. His love is conveyed through the hug of a child, the smile of a stranger, the hand-squeeze of an elderly acquaintance. His love warms us with the sunshine and refreshes us with the rain.

When you need a reminder of God's incomprehensible love, you need only look around to witness the many wonderful ways He lavishes it on you.

Feel His comforting, cherishing embrace. His love will not let you go.

Read Psalm 108:4–5.

Even though I can't understand Your infinite love,
I see it all around. Thank You.

A Sure Thing

Knowing where you are going takes
the uncertainty out of getting there.
Anne Graham Lotz

*D*istress. Disappointment. Disease. Death. Struggles in life can make our hands tremble, our hearts pound, and our knees buckle.

Until we reflect on our final destination.

When we know we're going to heaven, certainty fills our hearts as we look forward to the joy, beauty, and welcome that we know will meet us there. As we fix our eyes on our ultimate destination, we have the hope and courage needed to handle whatever comes our way.

The road you're on today may be littered with fear, anxiety, or worry. The future may not look or feel like a sure thing.

Look up! Heaven is a sure thing. God can be counted on. Keep going, regardless of the twists, turns, and unexpected detours on your journey. Keep going, certain of the One who saved you. Keep going, letting the picture and promise of heaven fill your steps with confidence and hope.

Read John 14:1–3.

Thank You, God, for reminding me
where I'm going so I can confidently face today.

The Glory of the Cross

*Suffering opens our eyes to the centrality of the cross
in the Christian life, enables us to lift up
the crucified Savior to the rest of the world.*

Elisabeth Elliot

*F*ew of us would voluntarily ask for a cup of suffering. Most of us get one anyway.

We are not alone. The cup of suffering has been drunk by generations of saints before us. Suffering is the very cup Jesus willingly accepted in life and in death. When we drink from the cup, we can allow the bitter aftertaste of suffering to overwhelm us, or we can have faith that God can use that suffering to transform us.

Take the cup of suffering you hold in your hands today and present it to God. Sit at the foot of the cross. Think of your Savior there, willingly dying so that you could be saved.

Through your pain and the faith you show in the midst of it, you are lifting up your crucified Savior to the rest of the world. Others see in you the glory of Christ's cross.

Read Isaiah 53:10–12.

Help me, God, to show Christ to the world in my suffering.

Pressing On

You may have no idea when or how God will answer
your prayers, but don't stop praying.

Nancy DeMoss Wolgemuth

When it feels like our prayers are being met with silence, we experience great discouragement. When we've talked to God for a long time and haven't seen any impact from our prayers, it's easy to become weary or to decide that God just isn't going to get involved with this situation at all.

Waiting days, weeks, years for God to answer tempts us to give up. It's quite different from "waiting" in our culture of instant gratification, where problems are solved within a sixty-minute TV show.

The truth is, we don't know when or how any of our prayers will be answered. What we *do* know is that God promises to answer. So we keep praying, for in those deep conversations with God, we are forging deep trust and developing strong faith.

No matter how silent God seems, dear sister, don't stop praying.

Read Psalm 13.

. . . .

God, give me the endurance to keep praying,
for I know You will answer.

Mama Always Said . . .

"Wherever you are, God is there," Mama always said.
"He'll meet you wherever you are."

Ronda Rich

What did your mama always say? Or your grandmother? Or that teacher who inspired you? If you're lucky, someone along your journey took the time to impart his or her wisdom to you.

Ronda Rich's mom wanted her to remember that wherever she went, God was there. It sounds almost mundane until we think about it.

In the days of joy and thankfulness, God is there. In the time of sorrow and grief, God is there. When worry assails us, God is there. When temptation entices us, God is there. When uncertainty tears us apart, God is there.

The great I Am is rejoicing, sorrowing, comforting, guiding, strengthening. He is walking with you. He is willing to carry the burden when it gets too heavy.

Do you need Him today, but feel you need to "get in a better place" first? No matter what your circumstances, He'll meet you wherever you are.

Read Psalm 37:23–24.

Thank You that wherever I am, Lord, You are there.

Trembling Faith

*The faith that gets us through unthinkable circumstances begins
with being flat-out needy and allowing God's love
to wrap us up, hold us close, and dry our tears.*

Carol Kent

*H*as it happened to you yet? Have you experienced something so painful that you never would have believed you could survive? If not, surely you've marveled at someone who has endured unthinkable circumstances, faith intact.

Faith borne of desperation is a strong faith—a faith that can get us through. When the pain is too immense or the trial insurmountable, we know we can't do it alone. At that point, we come to a crossroads. We can choose to give up, to continue flailing and fighting in our own strength, or surrender to the One who is *able* to carry us through. We come to Him with our trembling faith and our complete neediness.

And that's okay with Him.

When it's all just too much to bear, allow God's love to wrap you up, hold you close, and dry your tears.

Read Psalm 6:6–9.

. . . .

*I am so grateful for Your love, Lord.
Please hold me close and dry my tears.*

Wise Investments

Make an investment that lasts longer than a lifetime.

Brenda Nixon

*F*inancial counselors warn that those who hoard their money fail to build a strong nest egg. So, they advise diversifying one's investments to secure strong future returns.

You may not have worldly wealth, and your nest egg may be cracked; but still, you can use your personal reserves to make a difference in someone's life.

"What reserves?" you may ask.

Your prayers for a hurting soul. Your kind words of friendship. Sharing the love of Christ. Encouragement. A smile. All are diversified resources to invest in others. And an investment in others pays the highest dividends. Your life will be enriched in return.

The life of the Christ-follower is a paradox: when you give away, you receive. As Jesus generously invested in you, do so to others. Your godly reputation will last beyond your earthly years.

Use His gift of today to give to others, and your legacy will be valued for generations.

Read Luke 6:38.

Lord, thank You for today's opportunity to make investments that will outlast my lifetime.

Starting on Page One

*Beginning with sin instead of creation is like trying to read
a book by opening it in the middle: You don't know
the characters and can't make sense of the plot.*

Nancy Pearcey

In the beginning God . . ." Everything in life has God as its
reference point. The story begins on page one. And what is
this story about? It's about us. Where did we come from? Who
are we? What is the meaning of life—and of our lives? What
caused all this bad stuff that goes on in the world? What will
make it all better?

The answer to every question is all there, right in the
pages of His Word.

The world has big questions. Those questions require big
answers. Sometimes we worry that we don't have the answers;
we don't understand how it all goes together.

So start at the beginning, page one. It is ultimately the
story of God's love and care for the human race He made.
Read all the way to the end.

The grandest story of all begins and ends with God.

Read Genesis 1:1.

Father, thank You for the grand story of Your love for us.

Our Anchor, Our Hope

True, genuine religion . . . is the anchor of our hope,
the ornament of youth, the comfort of age;
our support in affliction and adversity, and the solace
of that solemn hour which we must all experience.

Abigail Adams

*A*bigail Adams understood that the Christian life is not easy. Affliction and adversity come uninvited. Sadness and darkness may fill many of our days. God does not remove those experiences from us; however, when we trust in Him, He offers great support and hope.

Like an anchor, He holds us firm when the waves threaten. He ornaments our lives, giving beauty and meaning. He brings comfort as we age, for our future is bright and eternal. He supports us in times of affliction and adversity when our own strength fails. And He will be our solace in that final hour when we leave this life and go to Him.

What love that He cares so much for us throughout our lives and then wraps His arms around us when our time on earth is finished. Such a wonderful God we have!

Read Hebrews 6:18–20.

Father, life can be hard, but You are my anchor,
my support, my comfort.

Wiping the Slate

*Only the Lord forgets sin. Only God can take it
and send it as far away as the East is from the West.
Man remembers. Man recounts. Man condemns.*

Francine Rivers

Some people won't let it go. You know the ones. They like reminding you of times you've messed up in the past. Maybe they've said they forgive you, but the next time a disagreement erupts, a historical timeline of offenses is unpacked, shaken about, and aired out—again.

People may do that, but God doesn't. The Word says that when we repent of our sins, they're gone! They have been removed as far as the East is from the West—in other words, they're in a void, can't be found. The slate is clean because God doesn't maintain records of sins confessed with a contrite and repentant heart.

People may periodically try to usher you through your Hall of Shame, pointing out errors and losses, but you don't have to tread the archives with them. If you've cleared your record with the Lord, no one else's scorecard matters.

Read Psalm 103:7–12.

. . . .

*God, thanks for forgetting my sins.
Help me give that grace to others.*

Seek His Face

We must learn to seek God's face and not His hand.

Joyce Meyer

*D*ad would come back from his business trips, and the first thing we'd ask him is, "Did you bring us anything?"

Smiling, Dad would tell us to look in his suitcase, and there we'd find them, gifts from his trip. It became such a habit that we anticipated Dad's return, not so much to see him, but to see the gifts he brought.

Does that sound at all like your relationship with your heavenly Father?

While God delights in giving good things to us, He does not want to be simply a Giver of gifts; God wants to be the Giver of life. He wants you to seek not His hands full of gifts, but His face full of love and protection and guidance. God desires that you seek Him for who He is.

Seek God's face today. That will be enough.

Read Job 33:4.

Father, I love You for who You are,
not for what You give me.

Eye to Eye ... with God

This love disclosing itself was no cosmic Creator
of a mechanistic universe, for the revelation was intimate,
personal. . . . God insists on seeing us one by one,
each a special case, each inestimably loved for himself.

Catherine Marshall

Stars too numerous to count. Fragile butterflies of breathtaking beauty. The laws of gravity and of the seasons. The rotation of the planets. The colors of a rainbow. The intricacies of a rosebud. Surely the Author of all this has a full calendar and a waiting list of at least a few thousand years.

But no. He created us too, and calls us even more beloved than the rest of creation, for we alone are made in His image. He insists on seeing us one by one. He invites us to be His own children, adopted into His family. Personally known by Him. *Beloved* by Him. We are "inestimably loved," as Catherine Marshall reminds us.

Look at the beautiful love-gifts of the created universe; read God's love letter; feel His delight in you. He desires one-on-one time with you. He's got it set aside. No waiting.

What about you?

Read Hebrews 2:7.

Father, thanks that I don't have to wait—You're always here.

Well Done

*Life appears to me too short to be spent in nursing
animosity or registering wrongs.*

Charlotte Bronte

"Well done, good and faithful servant." For the Christian about to step into eternity, no better words can be imagined. Whether your years of life number nine or ninety-nine, someday, time will seem short. How are you spending it?

Too many women are passing through the better part of their days wishing for a different life. They nurse animosity against those who have caused their less-than-perfect circumstances. They keep track of wrongs done to them. Life is just too short to waste that way.

Your heavenly Father has granted you a specific number of days on this earth. Today is one of them. Who knows how many more you have? Let today be focused on worthy things: accomplishing the work God has given you to do, loving others well, appreciating the lovely gifts of God.

Then, at the end, you will hear, "Well done."

Read Matthew 25:13–23.

Father, help me to use my today and every day wisely for You.

Now What?

*You never know what you might be missing if you grow up
too much and stop asking, "Now what?"*
Thelma Wells

Children are famous for complaining that they've nothing to do. Send them outside, and suddenly their day unfolds into an exhilarating whirlwind of friends and fun.

Children's lives have a margin in them that allows them to ask, "Now what?" They don't map out their afternoons around who they'll play with and what they'll do. They have room for spontaneity. As adults, however, we tend to schedule our time almost to the minute. No margins. No room for "now what?"

That's too bad, because God needs us to leave a margin in our lives for Him. He has people for us to meet. Places for us to go. Love to experience. Laughter to share.

What would happen if, once in a while, you left the laundry unfolded and left part of your day unfolded as well so you could say to God, "Now what?" What will He surprise you with?

Read Psalm 118:24.

· · · · · · · · · · · · · · · · · · · ·

Today is Yours, Lord. Now what?

Creativity and Light

We are meant to walk in the light,
and we have been groping along in the darkness.
The creative act helps us to emerge into the light.

Madeleine L'Engle

We were created to walk in the light, but too many of us are groping in the darkness. We hold out our hands in the murky fog of our lives, feeling unsatisfied, unfulfilled.

Our wonderfully creative God made us to be creative beings. Some of us have been given great gifts in the areas of art or music or writing. Others of us are wonderfully creative as we decorate our homes or cook our meals or do our jobs. We may find innovative ways to entertain our children or get through to our teenagers. Even mundane tasks are stirred with interest when we try them in a new way.

Discovering and using that creative, God-given energy is the key to finding our way out of the fog and emerging into the light. We take on a tiny bit of heaven, for the most Creative One of all looks down and smiles.

Read Isaiah 40:28.

May the work of my hands be pleasing to You, O God,
and help build Your kingdom.

Adventurous Living

The adventure of living has not really begun until
we begin to stand on our faith legs and claim—for ourselves
(and all that concerns us)—the resources of our God.

Catherine Marshall

*R*ecall those first days after high school or college when you moved away from your parents' house into a new place. It was exciting because of all the unknowns, but also a bit scary because you didn't have all the resources figured out.

What a wonderful way to begin your faith journey! You don't have resources of your own, you don't know what the future holds, you aren't sure how you're going to get from point A to point B.

And that's exactly how God likes it. When you stand only on faith and trust in the resources of God, *that's* when the adventure begins.

If life doesn't feel like an adventure anymore, maybe you need to do something that stretches your faith. The life of a believer—*your life*—should be filled with excitement as you continually stand on your faith legs and claim God's resources.

Read Psalm 143:10.

. . . .

Lord, I want to try out my faith legs and walk with You

Step Outside

To live circumspectly, within the safe boundaries
of either our homes or our churches,
ignoring the call to responsibility outside
is not to follow the command of Jesus.

Eugenia Price

We could probably do a pretty good job of living purely and kindly and graciously if we just didn't have to deal with one annoying problem—other people. *They* are the ones, out there in our world, who cause us so much frustration and anger and temptation. If not for them, well, we'd be pretty good indeed. We'd "live circumspectly," as Eugenia Price put it.

Safe in our churches and our homes, we can put up the walls and keep those pesky "sinners" out. Problem is, that's not what Jesus told us to do.

New life in Christ makes it possible to shape a nurturing home and a peaceful church family. And new life in Christ compels us to step outside of our homes and churches, to invite others to know the peace found only in Him.

We are called outside—where sinners desperately need a Savior.

Read Isaiah 52:7.

Teach me how to step outside, Lord, where people need You.

The Storms

God is in the business of giving moments of sunlight,
warmth, and joy during the storms
as well as speaking a final "Peace" to them.

Carole Mayhall

*L*ooking out the living room window, you watch the storm clouds gather in the west. Trees wave wildly in the wind. Big dollop-like raindrops splatter the window.

Then, a brief break in the overcast sky gives you a glimpse of sunlight. An unexpected knock on your door brings a wet, windblown friend with a thermos of hot coffee. The dramatic hues in the turbulent sky catch your eye like the colors of a treasured painting. The storm has a certain beauty all its own.

We often talk about how God will "work it all together for good," as if He only gets involved in our life storms at the end when He puts all the pieces together. Dear sister, He is there *during* the storm, always with you no matter how cold and wet and windy it gets. Watch for those unexpected moments of sunlight, warmth, and joy along the way.

Read Mark 4:35–40.

. . . .

God, help me to experience Your brightness in stormy weather.

Waiting with God

Perhaps among a host of other reasons,
I think God often ordains a wait because
He purely enjoys the togetherness of it.

Beth Moore

She remembers the words "Good news! You're pregnant!" as if they were spoken yesterday. For years to come, she'll speak of the morning sickness, the weight gain, the baby's first kick. Those memories will cement the bond between her and her child for a lifetime.

God longs for you to have a similar life-altering bond with Him. And sometimes, He ordains a time of waiting in order to accomplish it. Think about it—when do you spend the most time in prayer, talking with your heavenly Father? Most likely it's while you're waiting for an answer to a need.

God loves that kind of attention! He loves it when you spend time with Him.

So hold on. God will deliver you. And after He does, at every opportune moment, you'll speak of His mercies, His provision, His protection. And you'll cherish the memories you made with Him while you waited.

Read Psalm 27:8.

Lord God, bless our times together. I will wait with You.

One Choice

As long as there's a God, there's a choice. . . .
No matter what life hands us, we still have choice.
We can't always choose our circumstances . . .
but we can choose our response to them.

Janette Oke

When we were young, what seemed like complicated choices were really quite simple. Chocolate or vanilla ice cream with the chocolate cake? A red bike or a blue one? Lunch from home or from the school cafeteria? Other choices reflected our right-or-wrong beliefs. Cheating on a test. Gossiping about a friend. Being a bad sport.

As adults, however, our choices become more serious. Who will we marry? What job training do we need? Where should we live? Other, more troubling issues could follow: What do we do about an unhappy marriage? How do we handle a life-threatening illness? How can we pay the bills when we've lost our job?

We can't always choose our circumstances. We don't control life's events. But we *can* choose how to respond when facing those circumstances, those life events. As Janette says, as long as there's a God, there's a choice.

Read Proverbs 16:16.

God, may my choices bring honor and glory to Your name.

An Inch

Once we give an inch, God will take a mile.
He'll take a million miles. He'll soar on the wings
of the wind from heaven to here to show you who He is,
to embrace you with His love.

Joni Eareckson Tada

When we hear the phrase "Give 'em an inch, and they'll take a mile," it isn't usually a good thing. Too often we've been taken advantage of. No matter how much we offer of our time or energy, it seems that people always expect more. Give them an inch, and they'll want a mile.

But what happens when we give God an inch? When we open the door and invite Him in, He enters not just to visit, but to move in, to take up residence, to take *over*.

Beloved, that's a good thing. That means He is willing to go with you everywhere. He's there in the joys, the struggles, the darkest nights, and the brightest mornings. He is willing to go that extra mile not only *for* you, but *with* you.

Only then can He show you who He is and embrace you with His love.

Read Psalm 18:10–16.

. . . .

Thank You, Lord, for the blessings
You pour over me mile after mile.

Rebuilding after Loss

Those who were able to forgive their enemies were able to return to the outside world and rebuild their lives, no matter what the physical scars. Those who nursed their bitterness remained invalids. It was as simple and as horrible as that.

Corrie ten Boom

*B*itterness and unforgiveness don't hurt the unforgiven ones; they hurt the one who refuses to forgive. Persecuted by the Nazis who also killed many of her loved ones, Corrie ten Boom later learned that God would help her grant forgiveness, even for the worst of her tormenters. In the years after the war, she cared for others who, like her, had been imprisoned in the concentration camps, and she discovered that the ones who could forgive were free; those who didn't were still captives.

Whatever loss you have experienced—betrayal, financial crisis, suffering—you need God's power to move on. To start over, to forgive what may need forgiven, takes God's strength. Forgiveness does not mean you don't hurt or don't care; it simply means you want to move forward and rebuild. To refuse to forgive leaves you stuck in your bitterness.

God has better plans for you.

Read Matthew 6:12–13.

. . . .

Father, for Your sake, grant me the strength to forgive those who have wronged me.

Walk the Walk

Simple, sincere people seldom speak much of their piety;
it shows itself in acts, rather than in words,
and has more influence than homilies or protestations.

Louisa May Alcott

*A*ctions speak louder than words—or so the old saying goes. That's why humble people never have to trumpet their humility. It clearly comes through in every interaction they have.

Since many of us value conviction backed up by action; we cringe when someone talks the talk but fails to walk the walk. Some of Jesus's most biting remarks had to do with behavior of this sort. He easily saw through the veil of hypocrisy the Pharisees drew around themselves and cautioned His followers to avoid behaving in kind.

You want to live for Jesus—then *live* for Jesus. You don't need to talk about it or draw attention to it. You live for Him because you love Him. You walk the walk because you know it pleases Him. Your actions back up your words even when people don't notice.

And God, who sees in secret, will reward you.

Read Matthew 6:17–18.

Father God, I want to be genuine in word and deed.

Be Honest

He [God] wants us to call, to cry, to sing to Him.

Cynthia Heald

*G*od wants a relationship with us. That thought alone should cause us to stop in astonishment. "God? Wants to talk with *me?*" He does. Every day, every moment, in any way you might need to talk at the time.

You might call—loudly—in a time of crisis, knowing He will hear and come to your aid. You may cry—softly—over pain and sorrow because you need His peace, His hand of comfort, someone to dry your tears. You may sing—off-key perhaps, but sing nonetheless—simply because praise is on your heart, and the best way to express it is with a song you've committed to memory.

Come to God with everything you are and have. Share each victory, sadness, and fear with Him. Don't hold back or pretend; live honestly in His presence.

Call, cry, sing. It doesn't matter. Just communicate with your God. He wants to hear from you.

Read Micah 7:7.

Father, give me the courage to live honestly with You all day.

Something out of Nothing

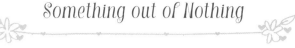

*We are very well aware that man cannot create in
the absolute sense in which we understand the word
when we apply it to God. We say that
"He made the world out of nothing," but we cannot ourselves
make anything out of nothing.*

Dorothy Sayers

We marvel at an artist's ability to create a memorable, soul-stirring piece of art. Consider the last painting, novel, or song that thrilled or inspired you. A work of that kind is unforgettable.

Many artists paint, write, or sing about what they see—the sights that inspired them to create in the first place. And these sights were first created by God. Only He can make a sunset, a robin, a baby's smile, or stormy ocean depths.

The creative act is an act of appreciation for the God who truly made something out of nothing. When we create, God takes our hands and helps us make something out of a blank white page, a canvas, a lump of clay, or silent strings on an instrument.

He then uses this act of creation to make something else—a changed life, starting with your own.

Read Exodus 35:30–35.

. . . .

Father, I create because You are the Creator.

Promised Forgiveness

Although we may not acknowledge and confess the sin,
there will be judgment for it.

Anne Graham Lotz

*I*t may sound crazy, but there are lots of women who don't get mammograms or have regular health checkups, even if they find a lump or aren't feeling well. Not because they're lazy or ignorant, but because they'd rather deny the affliction than face it. Once we have a diagnosis, a treatment plan, and a prognosis, there is no turning back. We must deal with it.

This can also be true of sin. *If we ignore it, maybe it will go away; and if it goes away, maybe it won't be a problem.* Bad news—everyone in the Bible who tried this approach proved this wishful theory wrong. Even when we manage to forget about sin and "move on" without confessing and correcting, we have only set ourselves up for the natural consequences.

Face sin head on. God promises to forgive, to cleanse, and to heal your wounded spirit.

Read 1 John 1:9.

. . . .

Search me and bring to mind unconfessed sin.
Make me pure again.

Showing Up

*It's not really important when I choose to meet God
every day. What really matters is that I show up regularly. . . .
Consistency, after all, doesn't mean perfection;
it simply means refusing to give up.*

Joanna Weaver

*A*s Christian women, we know that our daily time with God
is important. We might have tried different scenarios—
early morning, late at night, on the train to work, over lunch.
As life changes for us, so do our schedules. Yet one thing must
be on our calendar daily—a quiet time with God.

It doesn't matter *when* we choose to meet with Him. It
doesn't matter that while we used to be able to get up at five
o'clock in the morning, the sleepless nights with a new baby
have precluded that. Change the time to fit your phase of life,
and then stick with it as best you can. If you miss a day, meet
Him the next. Consistency doesn't mean perfection; it just
means refusing to give up.

Your time with Him is precious. You feel loved, you
gain joy, you come away refreshed and invigorated. And who
doesn't need that?

Read Luke 10:38–40.

. . . .

*Father, thank You that You allow me—and call me—
to meet with You.*

Fire of Joy

If you are what you should be,
you will set the whole world ablaze.

Catherine of Siena

*H*ave you ever asked someone, "How are you?" and received a long, sad tale of injustices? After such a response, you probably thought twice before inquiring of that person again. You may have even avoided the person so as not to hear their depressing daily report.

Yet how different it is when someone responds to your question with a cheerful outlook on life. Their confident and undoubting mind-set—regardless of what is going on—has the ability to lift your spirits.

These are the kind of people Jesus needs in this world. If we are what we should be, we are positive, uplifting, encouraging, hopeful people of faith. With that kind of attitude, we can, as Catherine suggests, set the world ablaze with the fire of our joyful hearts—bringing warmth and light to everyone we meet.

Read Psalm 68:3.

. . . .

Lord, let me set my world ablaze with the fire of my joy today!

Under the Circumstances

*His ultimate plan for our lives has very little to do
with our circumstances. Those are just the tools
He uses to transform us into a vessel He can use.*

Donna Partow

*I*f we belong to Christ, the victory is already ours. But why does life often feel more like a loss than a win? Why do our circumstances seem to roll over us like ocean waves, threatening to sink our little boats?

Our circumstances might seem to define us, but God would have us think just the opposite. He calls us to define ourselves as His children who are being transformed into people He can use. The circumstances are just tools to give us humility, compassion, understanding, grace, and other attributes that will help make us the people He wants us to be.

You may feel like you're sinking, like the waves are too strong for your little boat. But God is building a ship that can cross even the roughest seas safely.

You are never "under the circumstances"; you are sailing *through* the circumstances . . . with God.

Read Psalm 69:14–18.

Transform me, Lord, so that I am a vessel You can use.

Staking Everything on Him

A prayerful heart and an obedient heart will learn,
very slowly, and not without sorrow,
to stake everything on God Himself.
Elisabeth Elliot

The missionary wives' husbands were missing. Even as the women listened to the shortwave radio for news regarding their safety, they prayerfully carried on with household tasks and the mission work God had assigned to them.

Soon Elisabeth Elliot and the other women would discover they were widows. And they learned "very slowly, and not without sorrow, to stake everything on God Himself."

Sorrow is often the teacher that takes our prayerful, obedient hearts and draws them ever closer to God Himself. People disappoint, jobs fail, disaster and tragedy strike. The life we've been accustomed to disappears, and the pain feels like an avalanche crashing down around us.

It is in those times that we must learn to stake everything on the One who cannot change, on the One who keeps His promises, on the One who loved us enough to die for us.

God will take good care of your heart.

Read Psalm 108:1.

* * * * * * * * * * * * * * * * * * * *

As I pray and obey, Lord, help me to stake everything on You.

God's Strength

Whatever comes, God will give me
the strength to deal with it.

Lisa Beamer

Whatever comes." Can we really trust God that much?
No one is ever prepared for the unexpected twists and turns of life: hurt, betrayal, sorrow, job loss, financial difficulty, the sudden death of a loved one. No, the unexpected comes when we least expect it and, more often than not, it challenges our faith.

But God is here, seeing our tears, knowing our fears, and truly feeling our pain. Whatever comes, we won't go through it alone. Every "whatever" is in God's hands and, as Lisa Beamer discovered on 9/11, God will give us the strength to deal with it. He will hold us up when we want to fall; He will wipe away our tears; He will hold us tight and calm our fears.

When "whatever" comes your way, give it to God.

You can trust Him that much.

Read Philippians 1:27.

Whatever comes, Lord, I trust You to walk me through it—
today and every day.

Earnest Prayer

How great is the good which God works in a soul when
He gives it a disposition to pray in earnest.
Teresa of Avila

*P*rayer is a magnificent gift. Prayer allows you, a mere human being, direct access to your heavenly Father.

Prayer before meals is nice, but think of how little time it takes to do that: fifteen seconds times three meals per day. If our prayer life consists of praying only before meals, then we are spending less than one minute per day engaged in one of the most precious blessings of the Christian life!

Don't be afraid to pray—God isn't expecting fancy words or high theology. He is expecting to hear your praises, concerns, and requests. Talk to Him like you would a dear friend. The more time you spend in earnest prayer, the more time you will want to spend there every day.

You'll find that your time with God in earnest prayer is the greatest gift you have ever received. And the good He works in your soul will change your life.

Read Colossians 4:2.

. . . .

Thank You for this precious gift of being able to pray to You.

The Best Place

If God wants you in the place you are right now,
then there are no greener pastures.

Stormie Omartian

Sometimes we wonder if we are where God wants us. Circumstances seem to go from bad to worse. We struggle. We look across the nearby fence to greener pastures and sigh. If only God would send us over there.

Problem is, sometimes the pasture is greener over the septic tank. In other words, what looks greener from where you sit right now may not be the best place for you.

Consider what Stormie Omartian suggests: If God wants you where you are right now, there are no greener pastures—there is no better place for you to be. You may be in a solitary place with God as your only companion. You may be on a journey to freedom from a besetting sin. You may be among the unemployed or in a hospital bed.

Wherever you are right now, Jesus knows your needs. And He has you right where He wants you. Trust His reputation for taking care of His sheep.

Read Ezekiel 34:14.

Lord, I'm so glad You are my Shepherd.
I will trust in You today.

Just Be

*We have it backward. Our being must precede
our doing and consuming if we are to grow up
into all the fullness of Christ.*

Jane Rubietta

So much of our self-worth is wrapped up in the amount of activity we can perform in any given day. We don our Superwoman costumes and fly out the door, hoping to multi-task our way to true fulfillment.

Unfortunately, we often conduct our spiritual lives in the same way. *Do. Do. Do.* We want to feel some sense of accomplishment, so we don our SuperChristianWoman costumes and try to work our way to spiritual growth.

Jane Rubietta says we have it backward. We need to *be* first. We can be involved in church activities—which is good—but have we stopped to ask God if that's what we *should* do? Our very busyness often keeps us from the time we need to be a friend of God.

By studying His Word, we seek conviction, direction, and teaching by the Holy Spirit. With our renewed minds, our actions follow.

Read Philippians 3:8–9.

Jesus, help me be so that I can do as You would have me do.

Our Father

*When she heard the words, "Our Father," she closed
her eyes . . . and joined her voice softly with the rest.
Somehow it seemed to connect her safety with "our Father,"
and she felt a stronger faith than ever in her prayer.*
Grace Livingston Hill

What kind of father did you know from childhood? Was he the silent dad who watched you grow up from the sidelines? Maybe he was a dad you were never able to please. Or was he the type who delighted in you no matter what? Maybe he was the absent dad, never there when you needed him most.

Memories of our earthly fathers tend toward either treasured moments or painful scars. No matter what your paternal experience has been, your heavenly Father invites you with open arms to climb onto His lap and call Him "Daddy."

He is a Father who is always near at hand, who is always ready to listen, who offers us the wisest advice, and who loves us dearly and patiently.

Come to Him, child. Your Father loves you.

Read Romans 8:15.

Father, Daddy, thank You for Your constant presence and love.

Ever Available

I realized that out in my future somewhere might
be other sorrows. . . . But there was also the sure knowledge
that I need never meet any future difficulty alone,
that help from a loving God would ever be available.

Catherine Marshall

*H*ow reliable is our Lord! Every time we have our heart wounded, find ourselves stranded, or face great difficulty, God is there to bandage us, soothe us, and help us find our way. He is a faithful Father—we know that. But what we may not realize is that through each painful experience, God is building His credibility with us for our future difficulties.

Just like a child learns that her mom will be there when she falls off the bike or gets bullied at school, our heavenly Father is there for us. We learn through our daily challenges that God can be trusted, not only with little skirmishes, but also with the great big battles.

This is the assurance that Catherine Marshall draws from for strength to step forward into the future. Although more sorrows may be ahead for us, we can be confident God will be with us every step of the way. His help is ever available.

Read Isaiah 66:13.

. . . .

Trustworthy Savior, teach me to relax in my situations
knowing You are in charge.

He Is Willing

Prayer is not overcoming God's reluctance.
It is laying hold of His willingness.
Julian of Norwich

God is waiting to bless us, but too often we bring our prayers to Him like attorneys presenting a case. We feel we need to *convince* God in order to overcome His reluctance.

Just the opposite. Prayer is laying hold of God's willingness. His plan for each of us is as different as our fingerprints; therefore, His answers and blessings will be according to our specific needs in alignment with His will.

Praying for blessing isn't a selfish act; it is asking God to infuse your life with everything He has always wanted to give you but was only waiting for you to request.

God is not reluctant to give you what you need. He is eager for you to receive His gifts with gratitude. You need only be willing.

He can't wait to see what you'll do with those gifts!

Read James 4:2.

I pray for Your blessings on my life, Lord,
that I might use them for You.

From Within

*If you're generous with other people, they will
be generous with you, and that alone will bring you
unspeakable joy. Joy starts inside yourself.
You can't expect to get it from somebody else first.*

Luci Swindoll

Walking down the street, you encounter a child who is obviously hungry and thirsty. Do you wait for the child to pluck a daisy from a nearby garden or offer you some other token of affection before you extend a helping hand? Of course not. This child's need compels you toward generosity. The reward comes in the form of a relieved and grateful smile beaming up at you. At that moment, a feeling of delight and satisfaction envelops you.

There are times when a *feeling* of joy eludes us and the reality is that we'd be stuck in joylessness if we waited for someone else to deliver it. On these difficult days, our best guarantee of recapturing joy is to first take it to someone else.

You desire joy? It's already there inside you—a gift from the Holy Spirit. Go spread it around. You'll discover that joy was there all along.

Read Nehemiah 8:10.

Fill me with Your joy, Lord, and help me share it with others.

A Parent's Discipline

*What strikes me now is that in the many ways Mother
built our relationship, she illustrated the way God deals
with us as children. God knows and loves us completely.
As was true of Mother, God loves us when He corrects us.*

Ruth Bell Graham

A s any mother knows, discipline is one of the toughest aspects of love. Although seldom appreciated when administered, discipline is the seed that produces the flower of good character. Rare is the person of integrity who hasn't experienced discipline of some sort. It is an important teaching tool.

When it comes to discipline, God is the expert. He can't be persuaded or sweet-talked out of correcting His children. If discipline is called for, He patiently measures it out and persists until His children learn the lessons they were meant to learn. He endures the grumbling or sullen anger His correction sometimes inspires, knowing the good that will result if only His child will listen and learn.

God loves us when He corrects us. If He didn't care, He wouldn't bother. He wants us to be the very best we can be—and sometimes we just need a little help along the way.

Read Proverbs 3:11–12.

. . . .

Thank You, Lord, that You care enough to discipline me.

Sparkle

None of us should be like anyone else.
Each of us should be the facet of the Lord
that He intends us to be.

Joyce Meyer

"A diamond is forever," making it the perfect gem for an engagement ring meant to symbolize "I choose you forever." With facets cut carefully by a diamond cutter, each stone has its own unique quality. The suitor finds a stone that sparkles just the way he wants it and a setting that complements it perfectly. This is what he will place on his beloved's finger. He choses it just for her.

Dear sister, you are like a facet in a priceless diamond. You have a glimmer all your own. The Lord "cut" you perfectly, like no other. He has called you to sparkle in *your* family, in *your* church, in *your* workplace, in *your* neighborhood. If you don't do it, no one will.

Don't compare yourself to anyone else. You are the only "you" God created. Sparkle right where you are.

Read Song of Songs 7:10.

. . . .

Let me sparkle for You today, Lord.

The Strength of Weakness

Even when our heart is cold and our mind is dim,
prayer is still possible to us.
"Our wills are ours, to make them Thine."

Evelyn Underhill

She grew up in a strong Christian family and had carried her parents' values into her adult life. Though she was a caring, loving person, she'd never fully surrendered her life to Christ. "It took a serious marital crisis to show me that I'd been living a 'Christian life' in my own strength," she says. "In the process, my heart had become cold and hard. I had lost the joy. I had lost the will to serve. I needed to find a way to get back to God."

We have been created by God to draw close to Him, but we so often find our hearts cold and our minds dim. As Evelyn Underhill explains, even in those circumstances, prayer is still possible to us. We turn over our will to Him so that He can make it His own.

He desires our surrender, our prayers, and our love—not our efforts.

Read Romans 6:16.

My Savior and Lord, I surrender my "strength" to You today.

Out of the Box

God's not safe in the sense that we have Him in a box,
predictable and measured. We don't get to control
how God operates. No magical formula
assures the way God works.

Sheila Walsh

Our God is the Creator of all that ever has or will exist. We can't put Him in a box. We don't get to determine how He operates. We might *wish* to; we certainly would *like* to be able to tell God exactly how to run the world, but that's not our role. We are the created ones.

That's precisely why we will never fully understand everything that happens in our world and in our lives. We wish some magical formula would make sense of it all, but God, who sees the beginning from the end, often surprises us. His answers go beyond what we even could imagine. His blessings are more than we could request. His love is more than we can take in.

If God were safe and predictable, then He would not be worth worshiping.

Be glad your God is not safe, but that He does love you.

Read Isaiah 40:18–22.

. . . .

I never want to put You in a box, Lord.
Show Yourself big in my life.

He Is Working

The sooner we quit worrying about doing our part,
the sooner we can start rejoicing in the fact
that God is doing His part.
Jodie Berndt

*G*od is always at work. He never stops repairing, recovering, and restoring His creation. He never takes a day off, never just decides to take a break. Imagine if He did! The planets would spin out of their orbits; the seas would overflow their boundaries; the stars would fall from the sky.

We need not worry. God has it all under control. What a joy to know that He invites us to participate with Him in sharing His story in this world. He doesn't *need* us, but He *invites* us to join Him in the work. And even that task is ultimately up to Him—only He can prepare a heart to hear the message, only His Spirit can convict a wayward soul.

So don't worry, dear one. Do your part; God will do His. Take Him up on the invitation and leave the results to Him.

Read Philippians 1:6.

Thank You for inviting me to join You
in Your work in the world.

Salt and Light

You'll never ever satisfy everybody. Someone will always
have something negative to say. It's unfortunate.
But we're all called to a unique ministry.
We're called to be salt and light in our own way.

Yolanda Adams

When Jesus spoke the command to be salt and light, He didn't tell His followers exactly *how* to be either one. The *how* is up to the Holy Spirit, who leads each individual in a unique way. Yet sometimes we get caught up in thinking that there's one *right* way to perform certain ministry tasks. Jesus never expected His followers to emulate each other like cookies on a sheet. Each walk with Christ is meant to be unique.

Salt makes a dull life palatable. Light takes away the darkness. In both cases, we are called to touch our world in ways that bring life and light to those around us. And we won't satisfy everyone. The only question we should ask ourselves is, "Does what I'm doing please Jesus?"

He's your ultimate audience. Spread your salt and light. He will take care of the rest.

Read Matthew 5:13–16.

. . . .

Lord, help me to bring salt and light
into my little world today.

Follow the Leader

He will never allow Satan to discourage you
without a plan to lead to victory! Consider this carefully:
We may not always follow Christ to victory,
but He is always leading!

Beth Moore

*R*emember the funhouse mazes at the county fair? You and your friends would go in together for the sole purpose of trying to scare one another. Part of the fun was the uncertainty around every corner. You groped the walls to get a sense of direction and proceeded with caution, fearful of what might lie ahead. In the end, you knew you'd all escape, laughing at your fear.

But real life's not like that. We don't like the uncertainty. We don't like being afraid. We can't see what's around the next curve, and we feel lost and vulnerable. The enemy could be waiting to snatch us at the least wrong turn.

Fortunately, however, our Rescuer is waiting for our cry. He will lead us to safety and victory. He rushes in, pushes the enemy aside, and leads us out of the darkness.

Our job? Follow!

Read John 12:26.

. . . .

Lord, I don't want to meander fearfully in the dark.
Help me follow You.

True Beauty

In all ranks of life, the human heart yearns
for the beautiful; and the beautiful things
that God makes are His gift to all alike.

Harriet Beecher Stowe

What is beautiful to you? A baby's smile? The roar of a waterfall? The smell and taste of fresh blueberry pie?

We tend to think of nature as God-made and everything else as man-made. But ultimately, God is the Creator of everything—the new life that smiles up at you, the mountain chasm over which the waterfall pours, the blueberry that gives the delicious taste to the pie. And then He created human beings with gifts and abilities and senses to enjoy all that beauty.

God could have created a black-and-white, two-dimensional world with no sounds or tastes or smells. Instead, He gave limitless colors to flowers in the forest and fish deep beneath the ocean's surface. He gave us trees blowing in the wind and, yes, even the smell of blueberry pie.

All for you. He loves it when you enjoy the beauty He created.

Read 1 Timothy 4:4–5.

Lord, thank You for the beauty that surrounds me each day.

The Nature of Love

*The Christ-life in us, developed and set free,
will go by its very nature reaching out and spending itself
wherever there is want, in love and longing
for the bare places and the far-off.*

Isabella Lilias Trotter

*B*y its very nature, a river will flow from its source, at times meandering, at other times running at full torrent. Whether it cuts through the centers of thriving cities or wends its way through desolate prairie, the river is ever drawn toward its ultimate destination—the ocean.

As Christ-followers, we are like the river. Finding our source in Jesus, we allow His love, comfort, peace, and joy to flow outward from us to others we meet on our life journey. Whether it is our neighbor across the street or a hungry child in a war-torn country across the globe, we are called to exemplify Christ by pouring our very selves into the lives of others. The Christ-life in us will cause us to reach out and seek those in need.

The love of Christ in us will spend itself until, ultimately, we reach our final destination with Him.

Read Philippians 2:1–2.

*Help me, Lord Jesus, to spread and lavish Your love
wherever my life path takes me.*

Your Sustainer

The One who created you, who formed you—
body, soul, and spirit—is not only your Creator,
He is also your Sustainer.

Kay Arthur

*G*od created you . . . take a moment to breathe in that very
thought. You're not an accident, not a chance of nature, not
a result of evolutionary slime. No, you were expressly *created.*
God chose every part of you, every physical and emotional
detail, every gift and talent, and put the package together to be
delivered into the world at a precise time in history, at a precise
place, into a precise family.

But beyond that, He sustains you. He doesn't leave you
to fend for yourself. He wants to take those details, those gifts
and talents—that whole package He created—and use it for
His glory. He wants to keep you strong and vibrant. He wants
to draw you ever closer to Him, the source of life.

When you feel worn down, ask your Sustainer to refresh,
revive, and renew you. It will be His pleasure.

Read Psalm 119:116–117.

. . . .

I'm feeling a little worn out, Father.
I need You to revive me.

Hero

*It's all very well to read about sorrows and imagine
yourself living through them heroically, but it's not so nice when
you really come to have them, is it?*

Lucy Maud Montgomery

There comes a time for each of us when life calls our
bluff. We can easily parrot the promises we know from
Scripture—that God won't give us something we can't handle, that He will work all things together for good, that our
faith grows best in the times of testing. Then suddenly we
are bowled over by a betrayal that we never saw coming, a
tragedy that takes our breath away, a sorrow that won't let go.
All that we had imagined of our strong and heroic faith under
fire evaporates. We find that trust is hard work indeed.

Sadly, we often fail to live up to our own ideals, which is
why we need someone else who can bridge the gap between
who we are and who we long to be. Someone to live His life
through us.

That someone is Jesus. He will live heroically through
you.

Read Galatians 2:20.

. . . .

*Live through me in this difficult time, Lord.
You are my hero.*

His Word

To receive any deep, inward profit from the Scripture
you must . . . plunge into the very depths of the words
you read until revelation, like a sweet aroma,
breaks out upon you.

Madame Guyon

The Bible can seem like a scary book. We crack open the pages and just hope we'll find something we can understand; if we gain some insight and encouragement for life today, well, that's a bonus.

Madame Guyon would tell you to dive in. Plunge to the very depths of the words. Let them surround you, wash over you. Because God's Word is living and active, it makes its way into your heart. Like a sweet aroma that rises from freshly baked bread, the revelation will rise out of the pages. It will shine a light into your darkness.

Light exposes everything, good and bad. When you can see, you can clean away the cobwebs in your life. God's Word will describe how God's holiness can pour over you and rid your life of unhealthy relationships and destructive addictions. The brilliance of His Word burns away the shadows.

It all starts when you open your Bible.

Read Hebrews 4:12.

I'm diving into Your Word, Lord.
I want to learn more about You.

169

Shift Your Weight

Because God is firm and steady,
you can put your weight on Him.
Cynthia Heald

*T*o put your weight on something requires transferring trust from one thing to another. We don't walk out on a frozen pond unless we know for sure the ice can hold our weight. If we see the lines below our feet begin to spread or hear the unmistakable crackle of ice breaking, we know we are in the wrong place at the wrong time.

Putting our full weight on God demands absolute trust in Him. Too often, however, we're afraid that He just won't hold us. We fear the crackle of a situation out of our control. We shift our weight back onto ourselves.

God says, "Trust me." We never need to worry that He can't handle it, that we are too much trouble, that we would be in the wrong place at the wrong time. Trusting in Him is always our best choice, for He is firm and steady.

Read Deuteronomy 33:12.

O, Father, I long to put my full weight onto You.

Be Still

Be still, be still, and know that He is God;
be calm, be trustful; work, and watch, and pray,
till from the throes of this last anguish rise
the light and gladness of that better day.

Harriet Beecher Stowe

Be still. That's not easy to do when the boss hands you a pink slip or your husband says he wants a divorce. When difficulties hit, our immediate response is to take action, try to regain control, and fix whatever is broken. We become anxious, sleepless, and at times, even frantic.

And God calls us to be still? How, exactly, is that supposed to work?

God isn't calling us to inaction. But in the midst of our troubles, He is calling us to pause before we hit the panic button, to listen before we talk, to quiet our racing hearts before we give in to despair.

When we do find time to be still before the Lord, when we wait patiently for Him, we discover untapped resources with which to cope and hidden strengths with which to carry on. That's because God now is in control, guiding us, caring for us, and moving us toward a better day.

Be still. It's the perfect antidote to worry.

Read Exodus 14:14.

. . . .

Lord, I want to trust You and give my worries over to You.

Life in Christ

Where am I exactly? Already, at this moment, I am in Him.
And underneath me are His eternal arms.

Corrie ten Boom

Where are you right now? Maybe you're sitting in an over-stuffed chair, watching the snow fall silently to the earth. Maybe you're in a hospital bed, wondering what tomorrow holds. Maybe you're waiting for your phone to ring, desperately hoping for good news.

Wherever you are right now, you are also *in Him*. On the eve of Jesus's arrest, He prayed that, as He and the Father are one, so we, His followers, would be united to them. He wanted us to be one with Him, drawn close, inseparable.

Even in a Nazi prison camp, Corrie knew that whatever was happening outside and around her, she was safe in Jesus. His eternal arms held her tight.

Wherever you are, whatever is happening in your life at this very moment, you are *in Him*. And underneath you are His eternal arms. He will not let you go.

Read John 17:21.

. . . .

Lord, thank You that wherever I am,
I will always be in You.

No Greater Love

*He could not have shown you greater love
than by giving His life for you (John 15:13).
You can hardly resist being drawn by love, then,
unless you foolishly refuse to be drawn.*

Catherine of Siena

*A*n unexpected bouquet of flowers. A backrub. A chore done
to enable you to rest. When someone proves his or her love
through action, that gets your attention, doesn't it? Actions
speak louder than words. That's why, as Catherine explains,
there is no greater act of love than Jesus's death on the cross.
What more could He have offered beyond His own life?

While Jesus's death has the power to draw all people to
Him, each person must still, individually, accept that offer of
love. And some resist, seeing only strings attached to the gift.
Still others react out of cynicism or pain, unsure they can trust
without being hurt once more.

Has this love drawn you? Have you opened your heart and
received it? There is no greater love in all the world than the
love Jesus has for you.

Read John 15:13.

Jesus, I accept Your love and offer You mine in return.

A Practiced Hand

God's way of working . . . is to get possession of the inside
of us, to take the control and management of our will,
and to work it for us. Then obedience is easy and a delight,
and service becomes perfect freedom.

Hannah Whitall Smith

Some activities require the guidance of a practiced hand—one that takes hold of yours and leads you to make the proper response. This is helpful in the first awkwardness of learning to play an instrument, drive a car, or learning a complicated dance. But when life hits the skids, we feel so out of our depth that we have no clue what to do. We long for someone to take control of the situation and act on our behalf if necessary.

God guides us from the inside out, starting with our will, as Hannah explains. As we trust Him, the Holy Spirit moves our hands, our mouths, our feet. Our responses become His. But instead of being robots or puppets, ironically we have more freedom than we had when we acted on our own.

Need a hand? Take His.

Read Psalm 25:9.

. . . .

When I don't know what to do,
help me trust that You will guide me.

The Perfect Man

Women were first at the cradle and last at the cross.
They had never known a man like this Man. . . .
A prophet and teacher who never nagged at them,
never flattered or coaxed or patronized.

Dorothy Sayers

We look for perfection in those around us and are disappointed. The reality is that the people in our lives are far from perfect. They cannot be perfect for us any more than we can be perfect for them. So we would be wise to stop expecting it.

We should look instead at the One who defines perfection, the only human being ever to live a flawless life. Many people at the time didn't see it, but a few did—the women who surrounded Him as a baby, birthing Him, protecting Him, rejoicing in Him; those who surrounded Him on the cross, weeping and agonizing over His unjust death.

They had found the perfect man—he didn't nag or flatter or coax or patronize. He loved. He showed them their value. He taught them. He made them His disciples.

And they went out and changed the world.

Read John 19:25.

. . . .

You are perfect, my Jesus.
Thank You for perfectly loving me.

Begin with Silence

The fruit of silence is prayer. The fruit of prayer is faith.
The fruit of faith is love. The fruit of love is service.
The fruit of service is peace.

Mother Teresa

Tending to the needs of the sick, the suffering, and the dying, Mother Teresa shared the light of Christ with the world. She practiced five simple steps in her life, steps that lead to peace. Each step builds upon the previous step, and so step one is vital—we need to find a place of silence where we can commune with God.

Silence allows us to open our hearts to God, who longs for us to turn to Him. This is followed by prayer, where we share our concerns with God. Prayer leads to faith, which wells up in our hearts as confident trust in our Savior. This reassurance allows us to embrace others with kindness and to serve them. That kind of service brings peace. Like falling back onto a sumptuous featherbed, God's peace enfolds us and brings us in silence back to Him, to begin the cycle again.

Read Isaiah 32:17.

Lord, in silence I come to You to hear
and to serve and to find peace.

This Is Our God

*Sometimes God wraps His glory in hard circumstances
or ugly obstacles or painful difficulties,
and it just never occurs to us that within those
life-shaking events is a fresh revelation of Him.*

Anne Graham Lotz

Matt and Shelley experienced the tragedy every parent dreads. Their precious daughter, Malayne, came into this world with a myriad of problems. She clung to life for eleven days. Within moments of hearing her mommy sing "Jesus Loves Me," Malayne met Him face to face.

Later, Shelley said: "When God requires us to go through something we before thought unendurable, He gives of Himself to a degree that is nothing short of miraculous. He was right there! In my face, by my side, surrounding me. It was overwhelming. If I had to do it all over again, I would—if it meant feeling and experiencing the palpable presence of Jesus once again."

God revealed Himself to Matt and Shelley during what should have been their darkest days. They found Him to be all their aching hearts required.

That is the Jesus we serve. That is the Jesus we love.

Read Psalm 139:5.

. . . .

*Lord, I praise You, the mighty God
who reaches down to lift up His children.*

Celebrate the Mystery

*I think [Mister Rogers] made me less narrow-minded,
more tolerant, and more in awe of what's mysterious
about our faith. I think I thought I had my faith
all figured out, and he reintroduced mystery.*

Amy Hollingsworth

The mysterious part of Christianity is many times ignored. We don't understand it, so we choose not to think on it. How did a virgin have a baby? What was God doing before He made the earth? How did Jesus turn water to wine? The questions make us uncomfortable, as if our inability to answer them puts our faith on shaky ground.

We can't answer many of those questions—and we ought to be glad of that. What is the point of faith if everything can be explained, if we have all the answers, if there is no mystery left? God delights in our questions, and He will give us whatever information we truly need. Beyond that, we should simply be in awe of Him.

Let your questions lead you straight back to God Himself, and to your knees in worship of His greatness. Celebrate the mystery!

Read Hebrews 11:1.

*I stand in awe of You, Lord, and the mystery
of Your love for me.*

Master of Multiplication

Because of who He is, when Jesus touches anything,
there is blessing.

Rebecca Manley Pippert

*I*n the little boy's hands, it was simply five loaves of bread and
two fish. In God's hands, that same one-boy picnic fed over
five thousand people, with twelve baskets of leftovers!

We don't feel like we have very much to offer. Our
resources are limited. Our talents are few (and not really all
that great). Our time is full.

Like the disciples, the world says, "That's not enough to
make any difference to anyone." Jesus says, "Give it to Me."
Then He blesses it and sends it out to change the world—
maybe just for a little bit, maybe just for a few people. But
those few people in that moment in time feel the touch of
God.

You see, God hasn't changed. He loves it when His
children hand over what they have so that He can go to work
making miracles happen.

Read John 6:1–13.

. . . .

I'm glad size doesn't matter to You, Lord.
Little becomes much in Your hands.

I Wonder as I Wander

A wandering period can be a very real time of prayer,
trust, and faith in God—that He will provide, protect,
and guide us into the exact place He wants to put us
for our greatest development and outreach.

Luci Swindoll

There are times in our spiritual lives when we're not sure where we're headed or if God is even listening. Ironically, such spiritual dryness often comes after an event of great spiritual triumph or a spiritual "high." And sometimes it comes after a painful defeat. Either way, we feel alone in a vast wilderness with no oasis in sight. We wander. We don't know which direction to turn.

If you're facing such a wandering period right now, beloved, don't despair. You aren't lost or alone or cast aside. This is a faith-building time. Like any muscle, faith is built up through hard work and discipline. Taking steps in faith exercises that muscle. Continue to talk to God, even if you're not sure He's listening. Continue to trust that He will provide, protect, and guide—even if no evidence presents itself.

God is there even as you wander. He will bring you back. Soon.

Read Psalm 107:4–9.

Lord, when I can't sense Your presence,
help me see You through the eyes of faith.

The Fingerprints of God

Despite everything that had happened,
God's fingerprints were everywhere.
Karen Kingsbury

Our fingerprints are unique to us. Like snowflakes, no two sets of fingerprints are the same. We can't help but leave our fingerprints on everything we touch. The phone. The computer keyboard. Doorknobs. Papers. Books. We know our fingerprints are there, but we can't see those little invisible ridges that unmistakably say, "I was here."

God's fingerprints are like that. Although He is always present, always aware of our circumstances, and always hearing our prayers, at times we wonder. When situations spin out of control or head in tragic directions, we feel that God has left us.

At some point, we will look back at that time and, despite all that happened, recognize God's fingerprints everywhere. A word of encouragement, a flash of insight, a situation cared for in a way we had not imagined.

God's fingerprints are everywhere in your life. That's how much He cares.

Read Deuteronomy 2:7.

. . . .

I thank You, God, for watching over me and leading me
even when I can't see You.

Grace for the Journey

God is doing in each one of our lives something
expressly different than He is doing in another's.
He will give us the unique grace to bear our unique cross.

Joni Eareckson Tada

The versatile dough from a sugar cookie recipe can be transformed into as many beautiful shapes and designs as we can imagine and create. No two creations are exactly alike.

The same is true for us. We are not cookie-cutter people. God is doing something in our lives that is expressly different than what He is doing in the lives of our sisters, our friends, our neighbors. He is shaping us and our journeys, and no two journeys are exactly alike.

We often wish the journey was easier, our cross lighter. If we start comparing, we might decide that the cross we bear seems heavier and more cumbersome compared to someone else's. *If only we could trade places!*

Instead God says, "Let Me work in you."

The cross you bear is yours alone, but He will give you the unique grace to bear it. And one day you will lay it at His feet.

Read Psalm 138:8.

· · · · · · · · · · · · · · · · · · · ·

Fulfill Your purpose for me, Lord. Help me to grasp Your grace.

Stitched Together

God is the Divine Quilter. How lovingly He gathers up
the scraps and remnants and leftovers of my experiences,
my brokenness, and my joy. With the skillful
needlework of grace, He stitches it all together
to make a wonderful whole.

Lucinda Secrest McDowell

You don't have to be a quilter to appreciate the hard work and artistry of a handmade quilt—a lifetime of memories held in each stitch, each piece of fabric lovingly chosen.

Our lives are like a patchwork quilt. On the days when we believe we are a mess or at best, a "crazy quilt," God thinks differently. Somehow He fits each event of our lives—even the senseless ones or the painful ones we wish to forget—into a display of surpassing beauty. Faith in Jesus is the thread that runs throughout the handiwork. This thread not only holds everything together, it makes our quilt priceless.

Perhaps in heaven we'll finally realize why that thread of brokenness we believed so ugly was the perfect complement to the thread of joy. But for now, we can rest content that God, the Divine Quilter, is creating a masterpiece.

Read Colossians 1:17.

Lord God, I trust that You hold the threads of my life
securely in Your hand.

After a Fall

If, then, you sometimes fall, do not lose heart.
Even more, do not cease striving to make progress from it,
for even out of your fall, God will bring some good.
Teresa of Avila

*F*alls and failures *hurt.* With some hurts, we bear the emotional and sometimes physical scars for a long time. We are often left to feel that we no longer have any value to God—after all, we've let Him down. We could retreat and lick our wounds. We could find a way to blame someone else. We might just decide to never try again.

By the simple act of living our lives, we will fail once in a while. But even if we're at the ground zero of failure and feeling utterly humiliated, we're not to give in to discouragement. God knows our heart, and He certainly knows that failing is not the end of our usability as believers. He can bring good out of the mess we sometimes make of our lives.

Don't lose heart. God can bring good out of any failure. You simply need to trust Him.

Read Matthew 26:41.

If I fall, Lord, lift me up so that I might continue to serve You.

Welcoming "Firsts"

It is a constant exercise of faith for me to relinquish my children into God's hands. He is a loving Father, who loves them more deeply than I ever could.

Ingrid Trobisch

If you're a parent, you remember your child's firsts: first word, first day of school, first time driving, first job. Those events are major milestones marking your child's journey toward independence. But the fact that there are "firsts" also means that there are "lasts": the last time crawling once walking is discovered, the last day of elementary school, the last time as an unmarried kid hanging out for Christmas vacation.

Parenting is about releasing your children to step into each "first" God has planned for them, knowing all the while that you are preparing them to leave you. Your job is to work yourself out of a job—and it's bittersweet at best. As you surrender your children to God each day, you'll find the grace to welcome each "first" and "last" in your children's lives—and in your own. After all, He loves them even more than you do. Imagine that!

Read 3 John 4.

. . . .

I surrender my child(ren) to You today, Father.

Grow Strong

I challenge you to grow wiser, even as you
let go of the potentiality of youth.
Put meaning into the rings of your life tree.
Mellow. Sweeten. Lighten. Strengthen. Deepen.

Valerie Bell

*T*he years in a tree's life are recorded in the rings. The circles tell its life story, including years of plenty and drought. Count the rings, and you'll know how long the tree stood and grew toward heaven.

We count our years with birthday candles and gray hairs. But like trees, each passing year puts its mark on our lives. We too have lived through times of plenty and of drought. We have enjoyed the sunshine and gentle rains, and we have been battered by storms and maybe even struck by lightning.

We must continue to grow no matter what happens. We continue to mellow as we understand that no situation lasts forever; to sweeten, knowing that everyone can use a little kindness; to lighten, for we can help bear another's burden; to strengthen as we offer our strength to others; to deepen in our love for Him.

Read Psalm 1:1–3.

Lord God, I want my life to tell
a beautiful story of Your faithfulness.